NEVILLE ISDELL

with DAVID BEASLEY

St. Martin's Press

New York

INSIDE

Coca-Cola™

A CEO's Life Story of Building
the World's Most Popular Brand

INSIDE COCA-COLA. Copyright © 2011 by Neville Isdell and David Beasley.
Foreword © 2011 by Pamela Isdell. All rights reserved. Printed in the
United States of America. For information, address St. Martin's Press,
175 Fifth Avenue, New York, N.Y. 10010.

www.stmartins.com

Library of Congress Cataloging-in-Publication Data

Isdell, Edward Neville, 1943–
  Inside Coca-Cola : a CEO's life story of building the world's most popular
brand / Neville Isdell, with David Beasley.—1st ed.
      p. cm.
  Includes index.
  ISBN 978-0-312-61795-0 (hardcover edition)
  ISBN 978-1-250-00498-7 (first international trade paperback edition)
  1. Isdell, Edward Neville, 1943– 2. Coca-Cola Company. 3. Chief
executive officers—Biography. 4. Soft drink industry. I. Beasley, David,
1958– II. Title.
  HD9349.S634C645 2011
  338.7'66362092—dc23
  [B]   2011026763

First Edition: November 2011

10 9 8 7 6 5 4 3 2 1

This book is dedicated to my two families:

my parents, who molded me into what I would become;
my wife, Pamela; daughter, Cara;
son-in-law, Zak Lee; and grandson, Rory;

and

to the men and women of the Coca-Cola Company.
Without all these great people, none of this would
have been possible.

CONTENTS

ACKNOWLEDGMENTS

I would like to thank all of those in the Coca-Cola family who donated their time and memories for this project, including Jesus Celdran, Tony Eames, Michael O'Neill, Heinz Wiezorek, Jay Raja, Cynthia McCague, John Brownlee, and Tom Mattia.

I am also grateful to those outside the Coke family who helped, including Sam Massell, Jack Welch, Dale Herzog, Carter Roberts, and Carol Mastroianni; Georgia State University's Robinson College of Business and the World Affairs Council of Atlanta, including H. Fenwick Huss, Wayne Lord, Cedric Suzman, Tamer Cavusgil, Jacobus Boers, Jenifer Shockley, and Gary McKillips; the staff of GlobalAtlanta, including Phil Bolton and Trevor Williams.

The staff at Emory University's Manuscript, Archives and Rare Book Library also deserves thanks for its help with researching the papers of the late Robert W. Woodruff.

Thanks also go to my wife, Pamela, for her editing and guidance and to Susan Beasley, Zachary Beasley, Laura Beasley, and

Emily Beasley for their editing help. Finally, thanks to Phil Revzin for his early support of and belief in this project and to the very able staff at St. Martin's Press, including George Witte, Terra Layton, and Laura Chasen.

FOREWORD

This memoir, penned by my husband, is also about a life shared. You, the reader, might be as surprised as I was that my husband asked me to write this foreword.

During the past many months, as he wrote this book, he wracked my brains for the perfect person to introduce him, but he decided that this honor must rest on my shoulders.

I assume that part of his reasoning was that obviously I know him best. This must be true, our having been married for forty-one years and before that "living in sin" for two years in what was then referred to as Zambia, the small country where we met. We were considered very avant-garde at the time but it was the Swinging Sixties and so we were just ahead of the trend and have proved to naysayers that our relationship is a lasting one.

Even when I first met Neville, I knew he was the one I wanted to marry and as we got to know each other in those first weeks and months, I discovered his amazing work ethic, perseverance, and of course, ambition.

Over the years, I have watched him grow, but he made me grow also and rise to the occasion as well, and I believe that I was the soft cushion he could return to after a stressful day.

We realized early on that our personalities really complemented each other's. Neville is a definite Gemini. He is gregarious, fun-loving, and adventurous but on the opposite side of the coin he can be serious, compassionate, as well as stubborn. I believe that by being a quiet and steady companion I have been the anchor in our relationship.

This book has been enormous fun, as I have really relived our life all over again and found it fascinating to look back through the mist of memory and re-remember so many things. I must admit that I also shed a tear or two over the "lows," but they were few and far between, I can assure you, and we faced them together.

The lows were his constant traveling and focus on the job at hand, and I sometimes felt second best, but this helped me develop a very strong bond with our daughter, Cara, as she was my constant companion when Neville was absent. There were also wonderful highs: the traveling to countries and places that I would never have seen otherwise, basking in the glow of the position Neville finally reached, and the great financial rewards that have helped smooth the bad times and given us a golden life.

Reading this book has made me see my husband in another light: first as a young man making his way slowly up the ladder to bigger and better positions. Neville was always a very focused man, driven not necessarily to become CEO of the Coca-Cola Company, but to succeed at whatever task faced him at the time.

He was always excited with the job in hand and his motto was that he should tackle that to the best of his ability while looking for ways to improve the business and, of course, make his mark. He always said that if you fulfill your duties to the best of your ability the next step will come to you.

The journey with Coca-Cola took our family around the world. Whenever Neville was offered a new position, we would always discuss it in depth, and if it was in another country, we would get out the atlas and pore over the map, especially before we moved to the Philippines as I did not at the time know where they were. Coca-Cola always took great care of its expat personnel when they were transferred, and this was a huge help when facing life in a strange country, often with a new language to contend with.

The one person in our family who suffered from all our globe-trotting was our darling daughter, Cara. Neville and I had both been uprooted as children, moving from Great Britain to Zambia. We both found travel exciting and stimulating but poor Cara was moved to so many different countries (she has lived on five continents and attended six schools), she found it very disruptive during her early life. Now, however, she is happily married, and she and Zak, her husband, have shared with us our beloved grandson, Rory.

In today's increasingly global business world, these are challenges many families will face. Neville and I hope that our story will offer some guidance to those facing similar adventures, which are fascinating but not always easy.

While reading Neville's memoir, I was full of admiration for the way he quietly faced the many crises and confrontations during his career that I knew nothing about. He kept his equilibrium every time.

One thing I always appreciated is that Neville would insist on taking his holiday every year, come what may. This was very important to him and our family, and we always enjoyed being able to get away and relax.

We had never expected that he would become CEO and Chairman of Coca-Cola, and had been looking forward to enjoying the rest of our lives together in a well-earned retirement when the call came that would change both of us and our lives forever. My main worry was over Neville's health, our relationship, and how this new challenge might change it and his ability to tackle the daunting job of running Coca-Cola. What if he failed? I would be left to pick up the pieces. Reason won the day and now I blush at the thought that I tried to keep him from this pinnacle of success.

Five wonderful years passed and I saw him continue to grow, become even more confident, and relish all the difficult situations thrown at him almost daily as well as thrive at increasing his knowledge of geopolitics.

I also learned to appreciate him in a different way. He was able to include me in so many trips, and it was a pleasure to know that he really wanted me by his side and considered us a team.

When he stepped down as Chairman in 2009 I feared that he would find it difficult to relinquish all the trappings that go with the job, but he took this in his usual stride and was happy to pass the baton on to our dear friend Muhtar Kent and bow out from the stage and spotlight.

Neville always had a plan for retirement: to be intellectually engaged and stimulated and to live to at least eighty with me beside him. Now I look forward to all these promises.

I hope you enjoy reading this memoir as much as I have enjoyed living through it.

—Pamela Isdell

INSIDE
Coca-Cola™

INTRODUCTION

I was happily retired as a senior executive of the Coca-Cola Company, living on the island of Barbados and playing golf regularly in the bright Caribbean sunshine, when in February 2004, board member Donald Keough, former president and a great leader in the history of the company, phoned. Douglas Daft, Coke's Chairman and CEO, planned to resign after only four years on the job.

Don was named chair of a search committee to replace Daft and wanted to know if I would throw my hat in the ring. There were no guarantees, but he was willing to let them know I was a serious candidate.

These were dark days at Coca-Cola. Daft's predecessor, Douglas Ivester, had lasted only two years before he was told on a runway in Chicago by members of the Coca-Cola board of directors, including Warren Buffett, that he no longer had the board's support.

Coca-Cola had languished since the October 1997 death

of Chairman and CEO Roberto Goizueta, who in sixteen years had increased the company's market value from $4 billion to nearly $150 billion. Yet, in the post–Goizueta era, Coke was losing market share. Nothing, it seemed—even thousands of layoffs—had been enough to get the company back on track.

Coca-Cola has been marketed as a purveyor of happiness. The word itself appears in many Coke advertisements. Yet in 2004, inside Coca-Cola's headquarters on North Avenue in Atlanta, there was little to smile about.

The U.S. Securities and Exchange Commission was investigating the company for "channel stuffing" in Japan, artificially pumping up concentrate sales to boost the stock price. The company was accused of hiring right-wing death squads to terrorize union organizers in Colombia. Deval Patrick, the company's chief counsel and later governor of Massachusetts, had submitted his resignation to Daft, he said, in part over the Colombia controversy. Patrick and another top Coke executive had clashed over other issues, each insisting the other should leave the company. Coke's hiring practices were scrutinized by a court-appointed task force after the settlement of a major discrimination lawsuit. And abroad, the European Union was looking into whether Coke had violated antitrust laws. The list went on.

As the board began its search for a new Chairman and CEO, there was only one insider candidate, company president Steven Heyer. He seemed a favorite since Coke rarely looked outside the company for its Chairman and CEO.

I promised Don I would consult with my wife Pamela, and get back to him within ten days.

Never before in more than thirty years at Coke had I been seriously considered for Chairman and CEO. I had never really aspired to the job and never thought it possible, even though in the summer of 2003 some company retirees (as retirees do) began speculating that Daft would soon be replaced. Some said they were recommending that I succeed him. I told them all firmly that I would not take the job. I meant it, and Pamela fully endorsed my stance. I was now sixty years old and financially secure. I had lost ten pounds in retirement, was physically fit, and finally finding time to spend with my family after decades of moving all over the world and working countless fifteen-hour days. After Don's call, Pamela reiterated that she did not want me to take the chairman's job, worried that it would seriously damage my health and disrupt our happy retirement. "What will happen to you if you fail?" she asked.

There had not been a successful chairman since Goizueta, and Pamela worried that I would be the third in the line of those who tried, but failed, to break the streak. However, as always, she promised to back me in my decision.

"If I do it, I will not fail," I told Pamela forcefully, but agreed with her about the stress. I had already experienced an amazing career and we were very happy in retirement. The real question was, "Could I live with myself if I turned down the ultimate challenge?"

The answer for this former rugby player was clearly, "No, I could not."

A week after Don's first call, I told a rather shocked Pamela my decision that I would do the job for five years. The game was on.

I had spent much of my life fighting battles for Coke world-wide, often in markets where the company had lost its way and was losing market share. Now I had the chance to attempt the ultimate turnaround and, perhaps, revitalize the entire company. Talks and interviews with all the board members progressed. The press portrayed Heyer as the front-runner and there were rumors that he even hired a public relations firm to promote his candidacy. My name was rarely mentioned but it was clear to me that I was the leading candidate.

Enter Jack Welch.

Welch is a business icon, having engineered the remarkable turnaround of General Electric and raising its market value from $14 billion when he became CEO in 1981 to $410 billion when he retired in 2001. A 1995 *Fortune* magazine cover labeled Welch and Roberto Goizueta the "Wealth Builders."

In April 2004, Jack married, and at his wedding he was approached about the job of Coca-Cola Chairman and CEO, the job I had been all but offered.

Jack said he would consider it and then left for his honeymoon in, of all places in the world, Barbados. He was only a few miles from me on the tiny Caribbean island as active negotiations with board members ensued. The thinking was that hiring Welch would energize the company and prompt an immediate spike in the stock price, and I am sure that would have been the case.

On April 28, I had just arrived from Barbados on a business trip to Edinburgh, Scotland, when I received a call from Herbert Allen, a member of the Coke board. Herbert wanted to know if I would consider serving as president under Welch for a year or two, after which I would succeed Jack as Chairman and CEO.

I refused. There were so many problems at Coke, a turn-around was risky, at best. I was willing to take the chance if I were calling the shots, but would not be another man's fall guy. Welch had performed amazing feats at GE but knew little about the soft drink business. I had spent my entire life in the Coca-Cola system, starting at a bottling plant in Zambia and working my way up almost to the top. Also, I felt our management styles would clash, even though I did recognize that to the board, this team seemed attractive. Jack had a real track record as head of a major corporation while I had only acquired CEO and chairman experience at the bottler level in Europe.

As I put down the phone following the discussion with Herbert, a man I trusted and admired, I turned to Pamela and told her it was over.

Then Welch, still on his honeymoon, started having cold feet.

"When I thought about traveling around the world, I said to myself, 'I already did this once,'" Welch recalled in an interview for this book. "For forty-eight hours, seventy-two hours, whatever it was, I thought about it. Then I woke up."

Shortly after I returned to Barbados from Scotland, I took the call from Keough offering me the job as Chairman and CEO, which would make me the twelfth person in the history of the company to hold the chairman's job.

Coca-Cola announced my appointment after the close of business on May 4, and I was scheduled to meet with employees at headquarters the next day.

Joel Rousseau, who had been Roberto Goizueta's driver, met me, Pamela, and my daughter Cara at the airport in Atlanta. It suddenly occurred to me to ask Joel if he had the phone number for Roberto's widow, Olguita. He knew it by heart and I called Olguita immediately, telling her I had just landed and was back in Atlanta.

"I'm going to bring the Coca-Cola Company back to where it was under Roberto's great leadership," I promised her.

At headquarters, employees assembled in the courtyard for a meet and greet with Daft, Heyer, and myself. There was a podium in place, but Daft insisted that he had ordered no speeches. Heyer agreed with me that we were going to have to make a few impromptu remarks. After all, this was my first appearance before the people I was going to lead. I spoke briefly, emphasizing my belief in the power of the Coca-Cola brand. "And it's all about you," I added. "It's all about the people."

That is what the employees were looking for. It hit the right note.

I was scheduled to start June 1, but first had to obtain a work permit at the U.S. embassy in Barbados. I stood in line before reaching the booth where I encountered rough treatment from an embassy officer who spoke to me through a bulletproof glassed window. Due to my height of six foot five inches, the microphone was positioned somewhere near my chest, forcing me to bend down.

"Why are there no Americans who can do your job, why do we need a foreigner?" the embassy officer asked me.

That was a good question, but not one for me to answer. "That was the decision the board of the Coca-Cola Company made," I replied. "They are all Americans. I'm sure they know what they're doing."

It was expected to take weeks for the work permit to be approved, so Coca-Cola dispatched a team of executives to Barbados to brief me on the state of the company. We were on the verandah overlooking the Caribbean, poring over documents, when I suggested we wind down over beer. Gary Fayard, the chief financial officer, watched the sun set over the blue Caribbean Sea and wondered aloud why I was willing to leave this peaceful place to plunge back into corporate combat.

"Are you mad?" Gary asked.

It was another good question but the die was cast.

The work permit arrived earlier than expected and so I was back in Atlanta more than a week before my official start date. Doug Daft had already left so I sat down at my new desk and phoned Warren Buffett.

"I am working for the Coca-Cola Company pro bono," I told Warren, reminding him that I was not yet on the payroll yet sitting behind my desk.

"I think that's a very good arrangement," Warren joked. "Why don't we keep it that way?"

I offer this book because so many friends have urged me to write it, but also for the lessons it may impart about the Coca-Cola Company and my role in rebuilding the world's most popular brand. I strongly believe the story should not be told by a disembodied voice. In order to fully understand me and the company, it's important to trace my career from the early days in Zambia, to South Africa, Australia, the Philippines, Germany—the amazing era after the Berlin Wall fell and the former Soviet empire opened—Coke's reentry to India and the Middle East, and the five years I spent as Chairman and CEO.

Coca-Cola, designed as a hangover and headache remedy, was founded in May 1886 by an Atlanta pharmacist, John Pemberton. Today, Coca-Cola is sold in all but three countries in the world: North Korea, Cuba, and Myanmar. Coke is a low-cost, high-quality product. As artist Andy Warhol once pointed out, whether the customer is a king or a bum on the street, the taste is always the same.

Coca-Cola is a ubiquitous company. Its advertising helped shape the modern-day image of Santa Claus. Coca-Cola is the world's second most recognized term, trailing only "OK." At the same time, Coca-Cola has a secretive allure. Only a few people know the ingredients. Even I don't know the secret formula.

Coca-Cola manufactures the secret concoction at a few plants around the world. It is then blended with other ingredients to form a concentrate which is then further processed into a syrup form and delivered to restaurants and bottling plants. Historically, Coca-Cola made most of its profit from concentrate sales to independent bottlers. But over the years, the parent company has purchased many of the bottlers. In 2010, the company acquired the North American operations of its largest bottler, Coca-Cola Enterprises. Coke now owns 90 percent of the bottling operations in the United States and Canada.

It would seem that Coca-Cola is, in many ways, the perfect company: it's profitable, sells a product available almost everywhere, and provides the customer with a few minutes of pleasure at a very affordable cost.

However, in today's world, that is no longer enough. As you can see from the controversies mentioned here, Coca-Cola is not universally revered, in particular among certain elites. It is blamed for contributing to obesity and diabetes, for destroying the water supply in India, and for countless other malfeasances.

"The more money we make, the less welcome we become," Coca-Cola chairman Paul Austin lamented in a March 1970 letter to Robert W. Woodruff, leader of Coca-Cola from 1923 until 1954.

Austin understood even then that Coca-Cola would have to do more than make soft drinks and profit. Multinational corporations had become targets, blamed for many of the world's problems.

Much is written these days about corporate social responsibility but I would argue that this defines too narrowly the challenge global companies face. As a college student in South Africa, I was trained to be a social worker but opted instead for a business career. I believe that in today's world, we should combine these two disciplines in a three-way effort with government and nonprofits to build a better world, thus producing a cleaner planet, battling poverty, and disease. I call this Connected Capitalism.

While chairman of Coca-Cola, I tried to move the company in this direction. It's a work in progress at Coke and most global companies. And it's an important movement, one which my successor at Coca-Cola, Muhtar Kent, has embraced. I believe it will ultimately define capitalism.

This is neither a typical business book nor a typical autobiography. It's really a personal narrative. So please join me on a journey inside Coca-Cola as we explore my life story and the daunting yet promising and exciting future of global business.

One

FROM ULSTER TO AFRICA

I was born in Downpatrick, a small town in Northern Ireland, on June 8, 1943, the only son of Protestant parents. My mother's family was originally from Scotland, my father's from Ireland.

My father, Edward Neville Isdell, was a fingerprint and ballistics specialist with the Royal Ulster Constabulary. Belfast was a shipbuilding hub and therefore a frequent bombing target in World War II. The police headquarters were moved to the countryside about twenty miles away until the war was over, so it was in Downpatrick where I first saw the light of day.

I was christened in a little stone church in Downpatrick built on the site of St. Patrick's first church in Ireland. My daughter and grandson would later be christened there as well.

Northern Ireland was then and is still part of the United Kingdom, but has a large Catholic population loyal to Ireland. The friction between Protestants and Catholics was palpable even to me at an early age. There were Protestant neighborhoods

and Catholic neighborhoods as well as Protestant schools and
Catholic schools.

My grandfather was a member of the Orange Order, a fra-
ternity dedicated to Protestant supremacy, and every year he
celebrated the Battle of the Boyne, when the army of William
of Orange defeated the Catholic king, James II. My father, who
maintained close ties to Ireland throughout his life, refused to
join the order. He had the somewhat dangerous view, which I
inherited, that Ireland should be one country but only through
democratic means. The "troubles" as they were called were
subdued in those days and would not resurface for two decades.
Yet I would encounter these types of human conflicts for the
rest of my life. The ability to understand them and get past
them was a key business skill that served me well throughout
my career at Coca-Cola.

My childhood in Northern Ireland was a typical one, solidly
middle class, with a large and loving extended family close by.
My paternal grandfather was a postal clerk. My mother's father
was a shipbuilding engineer honored by King George V for his
service to British shipbuilding. I remember clearly when a Nigerian policeman came over for ten days of training and stayed
at our house. At that time a black man in Northern Ireland was
really unusual. The officer gave me a fluffy little toy that I
called Calabar for the city in Nigeria where he lived. It was my
favorite and my first link to Africa. I also remember tasting my
first Coca-Cola in Northern Ireland, at an old tea shop with
bullion windows. It was considered an exotic drink!

During those postwar years there were still Jewish refugees
from the Holocaust living in refugee camps, and I donated some
of my toys to the children there. Gasoline and other products

were still being rationed and on weekends we sometimes drove to the Republic of Ireland, which had been neutral in World War II, to buy items hard to find in Belfast.

My father was a tall, barrel-chested man who had tried on three occasions to leave Northern Ireland, but had been prevented from doing so because he was deemed "essential" at the police department. Positions in Greece, British Guiana, and Sierra Leone passed him by.

Unable to get out of Northern Ireland, my father channeled his excess energy into rugby, a tough, hard game, with kicking, passing, and tackling, but no helmets or pads. It's often said that soccer is a gentleman's game played by hooligans, while rugby is a hooligan's game played by gentlemen. My father was the president of a rugby club and my uncle was also involved. So I spent many weekends with my cousins at rugby matches, kicking the ball around on the sidelines during the games.

After serving twenty-five years with the police department, my father retired on half pension and took a position in what is now called Zambia—then the British colony of Northern Rhodesia—as head of the fingerprint department of the Northern Rhodesia police. This was 1954. I was ten years old.

Finally my father had the opportunity to live abroad, but relatives and neighbors in Belfast were baffled at our move. I'll never forget sitting as a ten-year-old does in the corner of the room, as the adults, who forget you are there, talk. One of the family members said, "What are you doing this for? What about Neville?" My father replied, "I believe that by doing this I will be able to afford to give him a university education. I am doing this for him. I want him to have more opportunities than I had." That stuck in my mind. My parents were aspiring for me. They were investing in me. They'd been through a war and they'd lost opportunities as a result. The big possibilities had passed them by.

I was excited by the move, having always been interested in geography and nature, collecting leaves and pressing them in books, poring over atlases to learn the names of countries. Although my father had wanted to leave Northern Ireland all along, my mother, Margaret, was not at all eager to go. She was a very good mother and doted on me, but throughout my childhood she was never a very well woman, suffering from bronchial asthma.

On the journey to Africa, I saw London for the first time. En route to Africa, the ship stopped in Las Palmas de Gran Canaria off the coast of Spain. Flamenco dancers came aboard. There was bright sunshine and beaches. The exotic nature of it all hit me. We were not even in Africa yet but we were in an entirely different world.

Our first stop in Africa was Lobito Bay in Portuguese West Africa, now called Angola. There, I experienced the harshness of the colonial system as white overseers lashed black dockworkers with hide whips. My father pulled me away and said, "I'm sorry you had to see this, but this is the way the world is. And it shouldn't be like this." To this day, that horrific scene is etched in my memory.

Our next port of call was Cape Town, South Africa. We were told that if we were up at 5:00 A.M., we would see the most wonderful sight. It was January, summer in South Africa, and my father and I were up on deck. All of a sudden, through the early morning mist, a piece of wondrous land emerged from the seemingly flat sea. It was Table Mountain. The order of magnitude was stunning. Ireland had its beautiful green hills but here was a nearly four-thousand-foot mountain jutting out of the sea. It was the most beautiful sight I'd ever seen. I fell in love with Cape Town, in my estimation, one of the three most beautiful cities in the world. The other two are Sydney and Rio de Janeiro.

During our four days in Cape Town, we feasted on the sunlight, juicy grapes, oranges, and melon pieces with dollops of ice cream in the center that we purchased from cafés. I also saw the first signs of apartheid: whites-only signs on park benches. It was a shock, but at the same time, it seemed to be the natural order of this society. It didn't seem right to me, but I did not suddenly become a ten-year-old activist. I must say that I accepted it, but it did make me uncomfortable. After all, the Nigerian police officer had stayed at our house two years earlier. Why had he been able to stay with a white family when black South Africans weren't even allowed to sit on a white's park bench?

After Cape Town, we traveled for three-and-a half days on a coal-fired train to Northern Rhodesia. I stood on the metal railing between the cars for hours, looking at the varied landscapes including the bleak semidesert of Botswana, peddlers selling their wares, and women breast-feeding their babies. We passed one of the seven natural wonders of the world, Victoria Falls, which straddles Southern and Northern Rhodesia. Part of the great Zambezi River, the falls are a mile and a quarter wide and drop 365 feet to the gorge below. The spray can be seen for miles, which is why in the local language the falls are called Mosi-o-Tunya (the Smoke that Thunders). Everything in Africa, it seemed, had a totally different order of magnitude.

In Lusaka, the capital of Zambia, we were met at the train station by my father's former fingerprinting colleague in Great Britain, Paddy Greene, and his new wife. My father was replacing Greene as head of fingerprinting at the Northern Rhodesian police force. Even though Lusaka was the capital city, the train station had no platform, just red earth.

Our family moved into a brand-new three-bedroom government house in Lusaka. With its beautiful shiny concrete floors, the house sat on a half-acre lot that backed up to the bush. For the first time, our family had servants. And they would wax the floors with brushes on their feet and I'd slide delightedly across the rooms as a young boy would.

During the first nine months, we had no electricity, only candles, Tilley lamps, and a wood-fired stove. However, for a young child, Africa was an explosion of new sights and sounds: frogs, crickets, spiders, and loud thunderstorms. I was soon thriving in Africa, riding a bicycle five miles each way to a government school with a British curriculum, sleeping under a mosquito net, and playing sports.

Schools were segregated by race and gender. Racial segregation overall in Northern Rhodesia was not as strict as it was in South Africa but cafés, restaurants, and bars were whites-only. Whites and blacks could shop in the same retail stores, though the blacks tended to shop in different stores because the residential areas were separate. Many of the shop owners were immigrants from India.

Lusaka had a local newspaper and only one cinema, where we'd go on Saturday mornings for movies. There was no television. At night we'd listen to BBC News on the radio. On Sunday nights a radio station in Portuguese East Africa broadcasted the Top Twenty pop songs. Sporting events were available only on short-wave radio. Pocket money was used to buy the latest hits on 78-rpm vinyl discs. Within a few miles of the Lusaka city limits, the occasional lion was still to be seen.

Abject poverty prevailed. Most of the Africans in Northern Rhodesia walked around without shoes and wore ragged clothing. Yet in many ways, the poverty was not as severe then as it is today in some parts of Africa, a result of the displacement or migration of so many people from rural areas to the desperate slums of the cities.

I was amazed by the friendliness and happiness of the people in Northern Rhodesia, despite their poverty. They appeared somewhat content. It was a society that seemed to work, to be at peace with itself. Some educated Zambians, however, were becoming discontented and political rumblings for independence—which would occur in 1964—had begun. Yet even the process of gaining freedom occurred with far less disruption in Northern Rhodesia than it did in other African countries and was cheered by a number of European expats, including my family.

Many tribal languages are spoken in Northern Rhodesia, but in school Africans were taught English, and because of the tribal differences English was and still is the official language of government. My parents and I studied a little bit of Chinyanja, also known as Nyanja. We knew enough of this language to get by if we encountered anyone who did not speak English, but that only worked in a Nyanja-speaking area.

At school, I first encountered Afrikaners, descendants of Dutch settlers who over decades had developed their own language,

Afrikaans. During recess, we played a rough, physical game called bok-bok in which several boys would make a human tunnel while the other team tried to collapse it by jumping on their backs.

Living in Africa, though, took its toll. I suffered from sunstroke, dysentery, and eventually malaria. In those day there was no air-conditioning. Yet, I generally thrived in the new environment, as did my father, who loved his new job and quickly became active in the local rugby scene. More than anything, he was determined to train Africans as fingerprint specialists, something his white colleagues believed was not possible. By the time he retired from the Zambian Police Force in 1967, he handed over a department of twenty trained fingerprint specialists and his successor, his first trainee, later became deputy commissioner of police. At that time it was the only fully Zambian division of the police department.

My mother, however, with servants to do the housework and me away at school most of the time, was at first bored and homesick. She eventually took a clerical job at a government medical dispensary. She counted the days until the end of the first three-year contract, when we would return for six months of mandatory leave in Belfast.

In Africa, the entrepreneur first emerged in me. I grew maize in our garden, roasted it, and had the family gardener sell it to workers on their lunch break, with the gardener being given a commission. In many respects, he was my first employee and I could have "ordered" him to do the work. However, the concept of reward for incremental effort seemed right.

In the summer of 1957, we returned to Belfast on the leave my mother had been longing for. I was thirteen at the time and younger siblings of my friends in Belfast were greatly disappointed to see that after three years in Africa, I was not black, as they had expected.

After the first round of visiting relatives and friends I recall a dinner-table discussion between my mother and father in which my mother commented on how our family and friends had changed. I will never forget my father's reply, "No dear, it is we who have changed and we will never be the same again." How true.

In a sign of my growing attachment to Africa, I wrote a letter to BBC television complaining about a story on Lusaka that aired while we were back in Belfast. The show featured old footage of Lusaka, portraying the city as a dusty wasteland. "Lusaka looks much nicer than that," I wrote the BBC. "My Dad has much better camera footage which I am sure he will lend you."

My parents knew none of this and were shocked when the BBC invited me to appear on television, paying for my flight to London. In a June 30, 1957, broadcast entitled, "A Boy from Lusaka," I defended my new hometown and narrated film my father had taken of Lusaka. I was honored to appear on my own program. Prince Philip, Duke of Edinburgh, the husband of Queen Elizabeth, appeared just after me and introduced the International Geophysical Year, during which sixty-seven countries cooperated on scientific research. I thought I was in illustrious company as I was shown the set for the program.

Back home in Lusaka, my television appearance produced headlines and accolades from the city council. The mayor later presented me with a mounted reproduction of the city's coat of arms and a citation signed by all the councilors which read, "Your obvious pride in Lusaka and your display of civic mindedness have been noted."

I was in love with Africa, so much so that three years later, I decided to stay behind in Lusaka at boarding school when my parents took another six-month leave in Belfast.

I lived at the Gilbert Rennie School and under the British system was assigned a first-year student, called a "fag," who as part of an initiation process had to fold my clothes, make my bed, and run any other errands I might have. I played rugby, cricket, tennis, and soccer. At the time, I wanted to be a geography or history teacher, although a part-time job at a grocery store during vacations and a friend whose father owned a clothing store piqued an early interest in business. I was also placed in my first real position of responsibility as a school prefect and head of my house, of which the school had four, as a way to promote internal competition.

I graduated with honors from high school and was offered a scholarship from the city of Lusaka—in part because of my defense of the city on the BBC—to attend the University of Cape Town in South Africa. My life very nearly took a much different path, however, one that would have left me with the legacy of livestock thief, not CEO of Coca-Cola.

An initiation ritual at my college residence required first-year male students to appear in their underwear early in the morning with a live animal. It was performed in full view of the women's residence where the windows were filled with ogling females. All sorts of creatures would appear: dogs, cows, horses. It was a silly ritual but, nevertheless, a time-honored one. My friends and I spotted a few sheep in a pasture near campus and one night drove in a beat-up Pontiac to retrieve our find. The farmer had locked up the sheep for the night in a barn so we stupidly broke the lock and stuffed four of the animals into the back of the old car from which we had removed the backseat. At a stoplight, a woman who was standing there waiting to cross the road looked into the car and saw the four of us and the sheep, who were loudly complaining over their plight. Her jaw dropped at this very unusual sight and she was still looking stunned as the light turned green and we drove away.

We returned the sheep early the next morning—no harm done, we thought. However, some other students had been caught attempting to break into the zoo. The police, after apprehending them, told them they could avoid charges if they told who purloined the sheep. We honorably, therefore, owned up, without realizing we would potentially be charged with stealing the animals. Eventually, as this very serious process evolved, we learned that a judge dismissed the case. We discovered that the judge had also been forced as a first-year student to endure the same ritual at our residence and therefore understood our circumstances. Our only punishment was a letter from the vice chancellor to our parents. My father, a career police officer, was none too happy, but I had dodged a bullet indeed. The judge ended up being the doyen of the South African judicial community. I recently sat next to him at a dinner, and even though he is now in his late eighties, he remembered the incident, confirmed his role, and still found it highly amusing.

For the three years I was in residence at Cape Town University, I was a Pepsi drinker. Cape Town in those days was the one part of South Africa where Pepsi had leadership. The whole of the university was exclusive to Pepsi. Although I was a Coke drinker back home in Lusaka, this was the one time of my life when I was forcibly a Pepsi consumer. Even in those days, when I consumed a soft drink outside the university, I chose Coca-Cola, showing the importance of product availability. Cape Town today is a thriving Coca-Cola franchise, built by the Forbes family, which turned a very weak franchise into what is today probably the strongest and best-run franchise in South Arica.

In college, I played on the rugby team, having reached a height of six foot five inches. Rugby was my main sporting passion and for me a lesson in teamwork and life. Every winter we went on tour, playing all over Southern Africa, which promoted great bonding. Today when I am in Cape Town, I still meet whenever I can with my former teammates.

Sociology captured my attention and I decided to become a social worker. Qualification as a social worker required students to do practical work. For example, I was assigned to do follow-up visits in the shantytowns of Cape Town for burn patients who had been at the Red Cross Children's Hospital. Friday nights were drinking nights in the shantytowns and on occasion fathers would come home, get in a fight, knock the stove or lamp over, and the child would get burned. I would go in and conduct a case study to determine if the father was abusive and if the family would be able to stay together. I did six months of this intensive, sometimes heartbreaking work.

I was elected to the student council on an antiapartheid ticket and in 1964 became the editor of the college newspaper, where I wrote editorials against the government's efforts to get rid of the small percentage of non-white students at Cape Town University. Although the college was more than 95 percent white, government officials wanted to go further and make it 100 percent. (They never quite succeeded and today it is a vibrant multiracial college ranked 105th in the world and first in Africa.)

"The University of Cape Town was a hotbed of white opposition to apartheid," my classmate and rugby team member, Hugh Coppen, recalled. "It was at the time the most liberal education you could get in South Africa."

Coppen remembers South African security police sitting in the classroom of one professor, Jack Simons, waiting for him to say anything considered seditious, which he often did. On occasion he was jailed. Students would picket the jail and demand his release, recalled Coppen, the son of a white farmer from Southern Rhodesia (now Zimbabwe), who now lives in San Francisco.

My views of apartheid sometimes clashed with my image as a rugby player. Rugby was the national sport of the Afrikaners and I remember once in the bar of the main stadium after a match a policeman approached me and said, "What's wrong with you? We thought you were one of us." He simply couldn't understand how a rugby player, a member of the club, could oppose apartheid. "Be careful, we are watching you," he warned. Later that year, my house was raided by the security police who were looking for seditious material. They found none, missing my copy of Mao's Little Red Book tucked away in the back of an old bookcase.

On one issue related to apartheid, I was faced with a difficult moral dilemma. The government of South Africa had decreed that all dances on campus had to be racially segregated. The student council passed a resolution to halt dances until they could be opened to students of all races. The problem was that some of the dances were fund-raisers for a student organization,

SHAWCO, that provided a health clinic, low-cost food, and other assistance for the poor in Windermere, a suburb of Cape Town. I knew through my social work that this help was desperately needed. The protest would have hurt the people we were trying to help, while we continued our privileged lifestyle. I believed we had to find other ways to protest and I was among the minority on the student council who voted against the resolution to ban all dances. I was the only member of the campus antiapartheid organization to do so. I resisted peer pressure and went against the grain, refusing to increase the suffering of those we were trying to help. I am still unsure to this day whether I was right or wrong.

It was during my college years that Zambia officially gained its independence from Great Britain. I organized a party for the Zambian students at Cape Town University. At midnight on October 24, 1964, in the ballroom of a local hotel, with the British ambassador present, we lowered the British flag and raised the Zambian flag for the first time as we sang its anthem, "Stand and Sing of Zambia, Proud and Free." I am sure that the availability of free beer for impoverished students added to the sense of history.

Although I was training to be a social worker, I again began to experience the lure of a business career. Many of my friends at the university were from wealthy families in Johannesburg and Cape Town. Their fathers owned businesses. They lived in what seemed to me were palatial homes and arrived at school driving brand-new cars. I didn't have a car. I was now mixing with a different group of people. I felt a level of inferiority, sometimes a level of resentment at the financial differences, but more than anything, aspiration. I was a policeman's son, but I felt like

I could one day reach the same financial status of my classmates and their families.

In order to earn some extra entertainment money in college, I worked on Saturday mornings at a local clothing store. I was hired not because of any knowledge of clothing but because I was a minor rugby star. The University of Cape Town had many rugby teams, with different levels of competition. In 1964, I had reached a second-league team, but progression to the first league seemed unlikely that year since there were two players firmly entrenched on that team in the position I played at the time, lock forward. In my junior year, I was offered a spot on a first-league club, if I would leave the university team. The other team was not very good but it was in the first league. My father advised against it. "I don't think there is any point in being a first-league player with an inferior club," he said. "You know my dictum to you, 'Always strive to be the best.'" That was a lesson for life. It made it easier over the years to turn down job offers without even thinking about it from companies that were not of the stature of the Coca-Cola Company. My father was certainly the most influential person in my life.

After taking his advice and staying with the university team, and making the first team weeks later, I was chosen in 1965 for a team of players drawn from South African universities for a match against Argentina. This was a taste of true first-class rugby.

After graduation from college that year, I landed a job as a manager trainee at Edgar's Stores in Johannesburg and ran a retail store for about six months before an offer arrived from a Coca-Cola bottler in Zambia. It was owned by Maurice Gersh, a Lithuanian Jew who had fled to Africa to escape the Holocaust,

walking part of the way barefoot to Kitwe, Zambia's second-
largest city, and starting a business empire from scratch. At one
time Mr. Gersh was the mayor of Kitwe, a fact I have always
remembered fondly while discussing the close relationship I
believe companies should have with the communities they
serve. I had dated Gersh's daughter, Rayna, one of my early, great
loves, in college but our relationship waned when her older
brother married a Christian, sparking a family uproar. She later
married a Jewish doctor. Rayna's brother, Bernard, is one of the
world's leading cardiologists at the Mayo Clinic and remains a
good friend. I had originally turned down a job offer from Mr.
Gersh while I was dating Rayna, but now the way was clear and
not conflicted.

I arrived back in Zambia two years after the country had
gained complete independence from Great Britain. Zambia's
first president, Kenneth Kaunda, was both a socialist and a hu-
manist. He led a nonviolent independence movement that never
targeted whites as individuals, but did blow up rail lines and
power stations to create disruption.

Kaunda tried very hard not to be polarizing on race. He was
all about the human being. In 1959, when I was sixteen, my
geography master invited Kaunda, who had just been released
from jail, to our school in Lusaka, and we had lunch with him.
I expected a firebrand. Yet Kaunda was calm and balanced. I
remember asking him, "Why aren't you mad at us? We've had
you in jail." I can't remember his exact words, but basically his
reply was that we, the whites, were the ones who were making
the mistake, right was on his side, and there was no reason for
him to be angry. He believed that he would not be living up to

his principles if he were influenced by the anger of the whites who had imprisoned him. Retribution was against his principles.

My father also knew Kaunda, who as president of Zambia was named honorary head of the Irish Society and attended the St. Patrick's night ball every year, which my father organized as head of the society.

I was always sympathetic with Kaunda's movement, but there were periods of uncertainty during the years preceding independence. White neighborhoods established security patrols. My father would be on watch at night, patrolling just to be sure everything was safe and secure.

After independence in 1964, Kaunda nationalized many of the industries in Zambia, including the lucrative copper mines, but, fortunately for me, not the soft drink business. It was the beginning of the failed and often destructive era of African socialism led by well-meaning leaders, but later exploited by the less idealistic, often for their own benefit.

Under Kaunda, the retail business was reserved for Zambian citizens, but permanent residents, mostly whites who had lived in the country for ten years or more, were allowed to own wholesale businesses, a system that still exists today.

My first job was as manager trainee at a two-truck depot in a small copper-mining town called Mufulira. Cokes were sold to supermarkets, bars, and restaurants. My salary was $1,100 a year.

Noting that one of the two trucks was often idle because there was only one salesman on the staff, I asked my superiors if the company would hire another salesman. They wouldn't, so I offered to get my commercial driver's license and was soon driving a ten-ton truck, "throwing cases" on every stop and

adding new Coke customers. I doubled sales within a year. A
fringe benefit of the physical labor was that I kept fit for rugby,
and I was soon playing for the Zambian team.

At that time in Zambia fuel was being rationed, a side effect
of Britain's economic blockade of Rhodesia, which had announced a "Universal Declaration of Independence" (UDI) in
1965 in order to preserve white rule. In retaliation for the embargo, Rhodesia stopped rail shipments of oil and other supplies
from ports in Mozambique to the newly independent Zambia,
a British ally, and a base for the South African National Congress, which was opposing apartheid in South Africa.

In order to get enough fuel for our two delivery trucks, I'd
drive twice a week to the Congo border on dirt roads in the
dead of night with cash to pick up diesel fuel in forty-four-gallon
drums, an activity that was technically illegal but kept the Coke
depot running.

The hard work paid off and I was soon placed in charge of
an eight-truck depot in Kitwe and rewarded with a one hundred dollar cash bonus, nearly one full-month's salary.

Trying to expand the Zambian Coke market necessitated
amazing and treacherous jaunts on the road nicknamed the
"Hell Run," which connects Zambia to Tanzania and the Port
of Dar es Salaam. With the border to Rhodesia closed because
of the UDI, the Hell Run was now a main truck route. Small
grocery stores and restaurants popped up for the truckers. Coke
products were provided by itinerate vendors. I was assigned
along with a Zambian coworker, Sandy Mwila, to survey the
road to determine if we should launch our own distribution
system. So one morning we set out in a Datsun van, with two

sand-filled sugar sacks to stabilize the rear of the vehicle, for the trip to the Tanzanian border some three hundred miles away.

In 1966, *Time* magazine described the Hell Run as "the world's worst international highway" featuring dizzying, hairpin turns, treacherous sand, and mud. My wife has always accused me of driving faster on dirt roads than on paved roads, and there is logic to this. Driving fast on a dirt road means you literally fly over many of the ruts and corrugations.

The Hell Run was in such bad shape that driving fast became even more hazardous. Before the border to Rhodesia was closed, this road was little used. Almost overnight, it became overwhelmed with truck traffic. With the continual transit of the trucks, drivers often found themselves heading almost blind into the dust created on the road during dry season. At least it wasn't muddy!

Sandy let me do most of the driving and I must admit that as a passenger, I would have been petrified at the speeds I was attaining. Yet youth is blind to risk and I probably took too many, but fortunately suffered no consequences.

About 125 miles from the Tanzanian border we stopped for the night in a small town called Mpika. Arriving hot, sweaty, and tired, we checked in at the Crested Crane Hotel and found that that there was only one room available, even though we had booked two. And, there was only one bed! It was what you could call a queen-sized bed, but had been much used and was distinctly concave, sunken in the middle much like the inside of a bowl. This meant that if Sandy, who was a rather large man, and I were to share the bed, we would migrate toward the center with great rapidity. We asked if there was a mattress that we could put on the dirty concrete floor, but there was none. So we decided we were probably better off sleeping in very close proximity to each other for the night. Exhaustion is a wonderful thing because when we eventually got into bed I don't think either of us moved until the next morning.

The food was not much better than the sleeping arrangements. Before retiring for the evening, we went to the hotel bar for a Zambian beer and what we trusted would be a good dinner. The menu was rather limited and we both ordered steak and chips (French fries). The steak arrived looking rather gray and leaden on the plate. Our attempts to cut it proved extremely difficult, not because of the lack of sharpness of the knife but because of the leathery nature of the meat. Each of us managed to detach one corner. The battle with our teeth to make the meat digestible resulted in neither of us returning to our steaks for nutrition. Instead, beer and bread filled our bellies.

The next morning we decided to take another risk by ordering steak, eggs, and chips—very soggy chips!—in the belief that the steak in the morning couldn't be nearly as bad as the steak the night before. Yet when the steak arrived it looked familiar . . . the corners were missing. The eggs and chips, however, were nutritious enough.

Back on the road, we took a thirty-mile detour off the Hell Run to visit the memorial near Kasanka where the heart of explorer David Livingstone was buried, the rest of his body having been shipped back to Westminster Abbey in London. We also toured the sprawling estate, Shiwa Ng'andu (Lake of Crocodiles), built in 1914 by an English aristocrat, Stewart Gore-Browne. You can image our surprise coming across, in the middle of the African bush, this magnificent English estate with well-manicured gardens, a chapel, a huge house complete with beautiful teak dining room table, silver candelabras, and a library stocked with leather-bound literary classics. Gore-Browne, a member of the Northern Rhodesian parliament, endorsed independence in the early 1960s, causing a huge stir in British diplomatic circles. In the final years of his life, he pushed the British government to move quickly toward majority rule.

It was in Zambia that I learned firsthand about the often adversarial relationship between Coca-Cola bottlers and the parent company.

The manager of the bottling plant in Kitwe was Charles Hutchins, and he was really tough. When he lectured employees, Hutch, as he was called, would make us all stand up on our chairs. Imagine me, at six foot five, standing on a chair. That was his management style. He was a bully, and while it was effective in the short term, it was not a style I chose to emulate.

Hutch didn't like the Coca-Cola Company. Once, Coke sent in a newly appointed rep, Lionel Cork. Before Cork arrived for his first meeting with Hutch in Kitwe, Hutch told me, "I want you to come watch this." When Cork arrived, Hutch was sitting behind his desk, with me standing beside him. There were no other chairs in the office, so Cork had to stand, a clear message as to who was the boss.

As the company rep, Cork's job was to help the bottlers increase sales. However, help from the front office is not always seen as help on the receiving end. Rather than escort Cork personally through the Kitwe marketplace, Hutch told him, "There's a truck outside, help yourself." So Cork rode in the truck for three days, inspecting the local stores. It was a game. Customers were giving Hutch feedback about Cork, and Cork was getting a reading from the customers and the market. When Cork returned to say good-bye to Hutch at the end of the inspection, there was a chair waiting for him. The relationship had been cemented, on Hutch's terms, although in many respects, Cork had won. Later when he worked for me, Cork reflected on the experience: "There are many ways to skin a cat."

When Maurice Gersh hired me, the idea was that in a few years I would run the franchise. From day one my immediate boss, the sales manager—a rough and difficult man—resented me as a privileged upstart and was hard on me whenever he could be, even though he himself knew he would never aspire to hold another position. These are not easy situations but if you shine, you can always get through them.

In the spring of 1968, Gersh called me into his office and said, "Neville, I don't think this is right for you." I thought I was about to be fired. Yet Gersh continued, "I don't think this is big enough for you. I believe you can have a global career with the Coca-Cola Company." I was stunned. Only twenty-four years old, I had no serious expectations at the time beyond running the Kitwe bottler, which would have been a great life. This was not the last time in my career when other people saw more in me than I saw in myself.

The head of Coca-Cola in Africa, an American named Al Killeen, who had a passion for developing young management, was scheduled to visit the next day and Gersh had arranged for me to meet him. Killeen offered me a job with the other large bottler in Zambia, this one owned by the Coca-Cola Company, managing all the warehouses outside of Lusaka, all the way down to Victoria Falls, 300 miles east to the Malawi border and 200 miles west to the border of what is today Angola.

Within a short time, I was back in Lusaka, with a substantial raise, a company car, and a housing allowance, working for the Coca-Cola Company, an international business. My parents were still in Lusaka, although my mother was very ill. I was awarded stock options for the first time, but was never able to cash them in because they expired in the 1970s during a prolonged slump in Coke's stock price. Still, I was honored by the options as recognition from the Coca-Cola Company. And later in my career options would prove very lucrative.

Within weeks of my arrival in Lusaka, the most important meeting of my life took place. I was playing rugby for Zambia against a touring team called the Penguins. It was a big event for Lusaka with several thousand spectators. After the event, which we narrowly lost, I was in the main bar of the rugby club with friends and fans who were complimenting me on how well I had played. One was Colin Gill, whom I had known in high school (and caned for smoking, as he reminded me). Colin asked me if I had ever met his sister, Pamela. I had not. She had moved to Zambia as a child from Scotland. Her father was a government engineer and they had lived about ten miles outside of town. As her brother and I brushed through a crowd of people, there was Pamela, this beautiful blond in a miniskirt. She had gorgeous legs and a wonderful smile. As we talked, I was totally captivated, but knew I was due at a team dinner in a few minutes. Being very sure this was an opportunity not to be missed, I asked her for a date to the theater five days later. Off I went to the dinner with the opposing team, returning two hours later for the rest of the festivities, including a dance. And there was Pamela, standing alone. The rest was history! I had found the love of my life, the woman who was not just physically beautiful, but the most supportive and understanding human being you could ever meet. Without her and her support, my ability to succeed would have been severely reduced.

There was, however, a complication. She was married at the time, albeit separated, having returned to stay with her parents in Lusaka after leaving her husband in Rhodesia.

This was 1960s Africa and while the fashions of Carnaby Street had arrived along with the great music of the era, it was still a conservative society. When after a very short period we started living together, it was somewhat scandalous. In addition, I had arranged for her to work at the Coca-Cola Bottling Co. where she was secretary to my boss. In order to ensure decorum was maintained, she always called me Mr. Isdell in the office and we arrived and left separately, even though our relationship was well known. She later worked for me when I was promoted to marketing manager.

Tony Young, who was in charge of West, East, and Central Africa for Coca-Cola at the time, and was very helpful to me in my career, took me aside to describe how conservative the company was. "This will impact your career," he said of my relationship with Pamela.

I have an impetuous streak when facing criticism and I replied that if I needed to resign, I would. Tony, in a very balanced way, pointed out that I had overreacted, and that I simply needed to be aware of the facts.

In my new job with the company-owned bottler in Lusaka, I was constantly on the move, which involved a great deal of driving often on treacherous roads. I had been assigned to pick up Killeen at the airport in Kabwe, north of Lusaka, to tour the local marketplace. He was flying in aboard a company plane.

My car was being repaired so I borrowed a colleague's. With the border to Rhodesia still closed, oil was still being hauled by road on tankers. The constant leakage made the paved roads slick. The car I was driving slid off the road into a ditch and hit a tree. I was knocked into the backseat, and had to kick the windshield out of the car to get out.

Killeen, meanwhile, was pacing at the airport, wondering where I was. He eventually flew back to Lusaka, exasperated and perplexed that this young employee would stand him up.

By chance, in the first car to see me standing by the side of the road and waving them down was someone I knew, and he gave me a ride back to Lusaka, bloodied and suffering from a concussion. I was immediately taken to the hospital. Killeen's mood switched quickly from anger to sympathy once he heard of my injuries, salvaging my career, I believe. The car, by the way, was a write-off.

Touring the warehouses throughout my territory and looking for opportunities to expand, I noticed that the eastern section was vastly underserved. It was a three-hundred-mile section, with only thirty miles of paved road. The rest was dirt roads through the bush. Store owners would drive up to the nearest wholesale distributor and load their small vans. They were doing a terrible job at excessive prices. Coke products were not widely available in the marketplace. I made a pitch for a new warehouse bypassing the wholesaler with direct distribution to stores in the main provincial town of Chipata. The company turned me down, saying there was no money in the budget and to try and find another solution.

I proposed setting up my father, who had by then retired from the Zambian police department, as a distributor with a

warehouse in Chipata. The company agreed. Surprisingly, I was
allowed to own 50 percent of the venture. With bank loans and
some of my father's money, we rented a warehouse and bought
two trucks. One weekend a month, I would drive the three hundred miles of mostly dirt roads from Lusaka to Chipata, taking
stock and paying the staff. Coke sales in the region were soon
up 150 percent, which of course, made Coca-Cola very happy
and meant that in my sideline, I was earning a significant incremental sum.

Meanwhile, Pamela and I started a cosmetics business, importing a line called Rimmel from the United Kingdom, shipping stock by air freight into Lusaka to avoid the logistical
logjam created by the Rhodesian embargo. It was a strategy
based on Coca-Cola strategy: ensure availability. Rimmel grew
to become the second most popular cosmetic in Zambia, behind Revlon. I also bought a small painting company that spe-
cialized in redecorating foreign embassies. It was a steady, reliable
business because the embassy staffs changed every three years
and every new diplomat wanted a fresh coat of paint for their
offices and house. I soon found that the profits from the side
business were twice as much as my Coke salary.

In 1969, when Pamela, now divorced, and I went to tell my
mother the wonderful news that she had agreed to become
my wife, my mother could only say, "Well, it's about time, you
know. I didn't approve of the way you were living."

We were married on January 10, 1970, in Zambia, spending
our honeymoon at Lake Malawi, with a first stop at my Coke
distribution center in Chipata. My new wife waited in the car for
two hours while I paid workers, took stock, and counted the
petty cash. I certainly started my marriage the way it would con-

tinue for decades to come: a partnership combining hard work and adventure. At the Malawi border, guards detained us for two hours, hoping we would give them a bribe. Only when I told them a fabricated story that I had an appointment the next day to see Malawi's president, Hastings Kamuzu Banda, did the guards stamp our passports and allow us through.

In 1972, Coke offered me a job in Johannesburg, a move engineered by Al Killen. It was clear that this could likely lead to promotions worldwide, but that would be up to me. It was then that I had to make the choice: stay in Zambia as a big fish in a small pond or go global. I chose the latter, selling my side businesses, trading security for risk.

Before moving, Pamela and I decided to take a short vacation in Brazil for Carnival and while there received an ominous telegram informing me not to report to the new job in Johannesburg but to return to Lusaka. I thought I might have been fired and for the last two days of our vacation, we sat on the beach trying to think of anything I had done wrong. Upon returning to Lusaka, I learned that there had only been a change in my job assignment, and that the transfer had been delayed, not halted.

There were at that time restrictions on taking money out of Zambia. I discovered quasilegal loopholes around this. I had arranged for an Argentine rugby team to travel to Lusaka for a match with the Zambian team. Even though I had organized the tour, the Zambian team did not pick me as a starter, knowing that I would soon be leaving for South Africa. It just so happened that one of the Argentine players was injured in a car accident and they couldn't get a replacement. So I played for the Argentines, which really upset the Zambian selectors, particularly after the Argentine side won. Then something dawned on me. The Argentine players were all there with their traveler's checks, which I swapped for Zambian currency. We then took the traveler's checks to South Africa inside the lining of a camera bag. Also, you were allowed to leave Zambia with your personal car. I purchased a twenty thousand dollar two-seater Mercedes-Benz coupe, importing it from Germany to Zambia. I was legally allowed to take the car to South Africa, but I could not afford insurance. Since I was busy with the new job, we agreed that Pamela and her father would drive the car down. At the Rhodesian border, customs inspectors discovered that one of the books in our car was banned in that country. They threatened to impound the Mercedes, i.e. our life's savings, before being convinced finally to simply seize only the book. Later on the journey, Pamela, driving through bush, had to stop completely as the car was surrounded by a herd of elephants. After experiencing even more questions at the South African border, we were able to get the car safely to a parking garage in Johannesburg. Legally, I was not allowed to sell it for six months and I was not about to drive the car before then, starting it only occasionally to keep the battery charged. I found a willing buyer in Al Killeen, my new boss at Coke and the same man whom I had earlier in my career failed to collect at the airport. We used the money to pay cash for our first home in Johannesburg.

I would never live in Zambia again, but the move from Ulster to Africa was the making of me. It made me want to explore the rest of the world.

Two

IN JOHANNESBURG:
MY GLOBAL CAREER IS LAUNCHED

O ur move to Johannesburg took me from the small, sleepy country of Zambia, where the transition from white minority rule had been largely peaceful, to the economic capital of Africa, which was in the midst of extreme racial conflict.

South Africa had the largest, most vibrant economy in sub-Saharan Africa. Johannesburg even today is still Africa's financial center. Yet South Africa remained one of the few countries on the continent that stubbornly continued to fight black majority rule. The atmosphere in South Africa was so tense, that before accepting the transfer to Johannesburg, I had taken the precaution of having the company ensure that I would be allowed to obtain the necessary approvals to live and work there given my political activities at Cape Town University.

When I arrived, opposition to apartheid was growing worldwide and would explode in the summer of 1976 with the Soweto riots that killed several hundred people. As a young businessman, I faced the challenge of somehow succeeding in an increasingly hostile environment.

It was a difficult period and yet I look back on the next nine years in South Africa as my family's happiest time, marked by the birth of our darling daughter, Cara, in 1978.

My first job was as an assistant to the general manager of the Johannesburg bottling plant, the largest company-owned plant in the world. There was not a clearly defined role of what I was going to do. The job had been engineered by Al Killeen really as a training job, a first exposure to Coke's operations in South Africa.

Initially, there was a cold shoulder from the Afrikaners on the plant management team. These were white descendants of Dutch settlers and they viewed me as an Englishman, not an Irishman. The Afrikaners had fought two wars with the English and even decades later there was still lingering baggage from those conflicts.

My company car did not arrive until I had been on the job for three months so I was forced to drive around in a horrible second-hand model. When I wanted to get something done, the Afrikaners resisted, just to show me that they had a little bit of power.

A single rugby match broke the ice. I was playing for an English-speaking rugby club and two of the top Afrikaners from the office saw me play in a match at Ellis Park Stadium against their favorite team. The next day at the office, there was a completely different chemistry, with the Afrikaners complimenting me on my play and chatting about the match. My new car arrived in short order. Rugby is a powerful part of the Afrikan psyche. Nelson Mandela understood that, embracing the white South African rugby team shortly after he was elected president, knowing that this would help unite the country. That story is brilliantly told in the movie *Invictus*, in which the relationship with the team captain is one of the great human stories of leadership and reconciliation.

My first assignment at the bottling plant was to examine stock control. They had given me a tough job as this was one of many areas where incorrect numbers could be inserted in order to balance the books. In those days, most of the Coke products were sold in glass bottles and the bottles had great value. That's why retailers charged deposits. You paid a deposit when you bought a bottle and then you got your money back when you returned the empty. Inside a bottling plant, there was a certain amount of bottle theft, with employees stealing empties which they could easily convert at deposit value for cash. There was also a certain amount of breakage during the production process and also during the loading of trucks. My job was to determine what was actually happening to the bottles. And I dug deep, instituting strict procedures such as a daily weighing of breakage in order to calculate the number of bottles broken. After three months, I had uncovered a ring that was involved in falsification. Not only were some employees dismissed but losses were reduced by 60 percent. Considering that each day the plant handled nearly a million bottles, this was real progress. This example is just one of many that led me to describe successful bottlers as those who "chase pennies down the hallway."

Success on my first project helped cement a bond with the plant manager, Fred Meyer, a South African of German origin.

Further, similar projects ensued and after only nine months there was a major management shuffle which saw Ian Wilson, a South African who had been in charge of Coke in all of Southern Africa, transferred to Canada. He was succeeded by Meyer.

The new general manager was Neville Kirchman, and my new job was marketing manager. This was a huge responsibility and controversial, as normally the Durban or Pretoria marketing managers were promoted to this job. The marketing manager at Durban resigned when I was promoted (we are in fact still good friends), and this solved another problem since the Johannesburg general sales manager, who reported to me, also had his nose out of joint. He moved into the Durban slot. Neville 1, as Kirchman became known, and Neville 2 (me) soon built a great working relationship and he became another mentor.

I will never forget the first time I addressed the complete marketing and sales team at the Johannesburg plant in a packed conference hall. The senior 60 of 300 employees who reported to me were there and at the age of thirty-one, I was clearly one of the youngest in the room. Thankfully, I spoke from behind a podium which I needed to grab as my legs were like jelly. As I stood, my right leg shook, then my left one, and vice versa. This was a reflection of stage fright, something I have lived with all my life. It has improved over the years but I still suffer from stage fright. My executive assistants spot it by my frequent visits to the bathroom before speaking.

It was a seemingly uneventful but happy period of my career. In retrospect, these were very important, formative years. Luke Smith, then Coke's president, came down to Johannesburg for a visit and I proudly gave him a demonstration for a new television commercial on Tab, Coke's low-calorie drink. The commercial featured two attractive women playing tennis.

"You can't use that," Smith told me. I had no idea why but he pointed out that one of the women in the ad had a Wilson tennis racket. Wilson at the time was owned by Pepsi. I had no idea, but it pointed out the extreme competitiveness between Coke and Pepsi, which Coke execs in those days, even in official memos, called "the imitator." It also exemplified how isolated the outposts of the company were and how little we knew about the rest of the world.

I have had the pleasure of working alongside some great characters in my career. Bob du Plessis, one of the Afrikaners who had given me the cold shoulder during my first weeks in Johannesburg, was one of them. I had succeeded him as marketing manager at the Johannesburg plant where he was a legend, having risen from the ranks of salesman, and he knew every trick in the book. In those days, our major customers were not the supermarket chains which only then were emerging, but the corner, self-service convenience-style stores, open seven days a week, run by families, with a strong Greek and Portuguese representation. To his credit, in our handover, Bob had taken me around to the top one hundred stores, endorsed me, and briefed me on how to deal with them. The bottom line was to stay charming, stay tough, but every now and again give them a discount. By then, I had joined Bob's Thursday evening tennis matches at the flood-lit courts at his house. Sport tells you a lot about people and when Warren Buffett says, "If it's on the line, it's out," du Plessis would have said, "Only if it's the opponent's shot." Du Plessis is probably the only person I have ever played against who after double faulting, took another serve because he was not ready.

Du Plessis was promoted to head of marketing for Southern Africa. He was no ad guru but was smart and naughty. We had just launched a 500 ml returnable bottle with a resealable cap, a major innovation, which became a huge success. Du Plessis and I regularly had lunch together and on this occasion, he asked me to join him a few minutes early to review a presentation on the benefits of the packaging for the new bottle. The ad agency had sent him an advance piece of artwork which in no way highlighted the major benefits of resealability, but was lifestyle-based, and I quickly agreed with him that it needed significant work. Now to the agency presentation by the sort of smooth-talking, trendy people du Plessis had little respect for. He listened to the usual hyperbole and then very simply said, "This is shit. Don't you agree, Neville?" I mumbled an agreement while avoiding the expletive (not my language). The account executive made the fatal mistake of defending the work by claiming he was following the company's instructions. "I will give you instructions," Bob said. "You see that cap? That is what it is all about. You be back here in twenty-four hours with artwork that makes the cap stand out like a dog's balls. You got it? A dog's balls." As the ad agency reps exited in disarray, Bob yelled, "Don't be late." After the door closed, he burst into laughter. That was never my style, but you have to know how to work in a tough school. The ad was back the next day and the revised version clearly worked.

As marketing manager, I frequently toured the stores in Johannesburg, including the black townships such as Soweto. Under apartheid, black and mixed-race South Africans *were* able to leave the townships to work in other parts of Johannesburg, but they had to be back by curfew at nightfall and they had to carry a pass.

Legally, blacks were only allowed to drink one alcoholic beverage, a beer made from maize called Umqombothi. However, the law was largely ignored by the police. The townships were filled with tiny, unlicensed bars called shebeens, which were private homes converted into pubs. These drinking dens sold regular liquor, serving ten to twelve customers at a time. One of the popular drinks was whiskey and Coke. So we had a sales representative who worked the shebeens. Here we were hiring someone to promote our products, as the breweries were also doing, in illegal outlets, a clear example of how the business world operated in the real world of apartheid.

I wanted to get a feel for what this market was like, but the shebeens didn't really get going until after the workday was over, six or seven in the evening. Legally, I required a permit to go into the townships, and mine expired at 5 P.M. Occasionally I would stay past the deadline in order to visit the shebeens and talk to the owners and the customers. There I was, a white man chatting in the shebeens past curfew, which, technically, was illegal. Yet the people welcomed me and talked openly about political issues and how apartheid had to end. I was sympathetic to those views and was getting a valuable political education from these business trips.

On Christmas Eve 1975, a group of us from the office repaired to the Sunnyside Park Hotel for a wind-down. Christmas season is extremely busy, the December month accounting for 17 percent of annual sales since it is a double peak—summer *and* Christmas. Much of that heightened business activity happens before Christmas, so that night it was the year-end and we were celebrating a year with record sales. As other friends joined us, we became a large group, standing on the lawn overlooking the beautiful and wealthy suburbs of Johannesburg.

The talk soon turned to politics. Some, but not the majority, in our group thought there was tension in the air. By my third beer, I ventured that based on my Soweto visits, we were facing another Sharpeville, when South African police in March 1960 opened fire on peaceful black protesters, killing more than sixty of them. I was challenged with the question, "What are you going to do about it?"

As I looked over the rich northern suburbs with their well-manicured gardens and swimming pools, I said that the values of all the homes we were looking at would soon plummet and that I was going to sell my house and rent one instead, as I wanted to protect my gains in a strong real estate market.

This is not the kind of Christmas present one wants to bring home on Christmas Eve, although I did tell Pamela I was only thinking about it. However, by January 31, my house was on the market and the sale closed on June 2, 1976.

Four days later, Soweto erupted over a South African law mandating that half the instruction in segregated black schools should be in the Afrikaans language as opposed to completely in English, which had been the norm. There was outrage in the townships over this since Afrikaans was widely viewed as the language of the white oppressors.

I was in Soweto on June 6, along with one of our salesmen on what we called "route riding," basically observing what was happening in the marketplace while he went about his normal sales job. Demonstrations were escalating and a school boycott was strengthening with the mantra "No education without freedom." I saw a few groups demonstrating in the distance and then a very large group on a hill about a mile away. One shop owner suggested I leave immediately since these were riots and vehicles were being burnt. We still had a few calls to make and completed them without incident. Our normal route out would have taken us in the direction of the protesters, so we took another way out of the townships. We were met near the exit by a mass of South African police with riot-prepared vehicles. After brusquely checking my permit, they told me that it was a "bad day" and that I was crazy to be there. It was only when I watched the seven o'clock news that night that I realized what had happened. South Africa had changed forever as that day innocent lives on both sides of the racial divide were lost, and the isolation of South Africa really began. Apartheid was no longer tenable.

I only made shebeen visits every few months and on my next one, there was a completely different atmosphere. "What are you doing here?" the bar owners would ask me. I could feel the tension building. I would argue this at dinner parties, and my colleagues would counter that I was not really a South African and had no way of knowing the situation in their country. They had strong views about what black people believed and what the Soweto riots meant. Yet when I asked them if they had ever been to Soweto, they replied "no," a logical answer given the legal prohibition. It did, however, reflect the dialogue of the deaf. Many whites did not hear the true views of blacks and led themselves to believe that their evasive platitudes were support for apartheid. The reality was different.

The growing opposition to apartheid put Coca-Cola in a very difficult situation. Our truck drivers became targets of the violence and one was shot to death in a robbery in Soweto. I attended his funeral and as the only white person there, could sense a mixture of resentment against me and support for taking the risk. Eventually, Coca-Cola hired contractors to deliver our products in unmarked trucks to the townships.

South Africa was a huge and lucrative market and the company had a massive investment there. In 1974, a corporate movement was launched by Reverend Leon Sullivan, an African American member of the General Motors board of directors, to push for equality in the South African workforce. Coca-Cola endorsed these principles in late 1976, although the effort proved later to be too little, too late. In 1986, after I had left the country, Coca-Cola divested from South Africa as the government stubbornly clung to apartheid, despite the human and economic toll.

After two years in marketing at the Johannesburg plant, I was named head of marketing over all three company-owned bottling plants in South Africa—Johannesburg, Durban, and Pretoria—a promotion and clear indication of having risen to the challenge.

There was not much for me to do in my new marketing job since each bottling plant had its own marketing manager. I really didn't think my new job should exist. However, I was convinced by Alex Reid, former technical head of the Johannesburg plant and the new head of Southern Africa bottling operations, that he knew nothing about marketing and that part of my job was to help him understand that part of the business, which I did. After about eight months, however, I felt as if I was becoming an impediment. Anything that needed to be done in marketing had to go through me before it went to the Coca-

Cola Company. I wasn't happy being unproductive, in a way pretending to work, and I wrote a memo to Alex asking him to abolish my job. Many people spend their lives writing reports, but not actually accomplishing anything. I wanted something to show for my work. Alex agreed and for the first time, I moved to the franchisor side of the Coca-Cola Company as deputy marketing manager for Southern Africa, based in Johannesburg.

Again, I was in a rather awkward position: I was the only person reporting to the head of marketing. Everyone else in the office—the heads of advertising, sales promotion, and market research—reported to me. It was just a transitional job, however, since Coke had decided to send me to a fifteen-week management course at Harvard University. On my return, I was to become the full-fledged marketing manager for the Southern Africa division, another big move for me.

Just before I left for Harvard, my father died in Northern Ireland, having returned there from Zambia. My mother had preceded him in death. After my mother died, my father had married the widow of Paddy Greene, his colleague who met us at the train station in 1954 when we first arrived in Zambia. Paddy had died of a heart attack at a young age and my father helped raise his two sons, who were like younger brothers to me rather than stepbrothers. We are still close, and I am godfather to Marie, my stepniece.

I spent the fall of 1976 at Harvard Business School, only my second visit to the United States, the first being a training trip to Atlanta earlier that year. I was immediately impressed with the size and sophistication of America. Harvard was a clear step up for me into a world I knew nothing about. I had to take a crash course in accounting and finance as this was not an area where I had any training. Although I had "kept" the books for our businesses in Zambia, I was self-taught as it were.

I was the youngest person in the Harvard course and the qualifications and experience of my peers put me in the shade. Most were specialists who were being promoted into general management. One of my classmates, for example, was chief engineer for Missouri Pacific Railroad.

For me, the Program for Management Development was a turning point and while no one, I am sure, ever saw me as a future CEO of Coca-Cola, I would put myself first in the class of those who learned the most, having entered knowing that I was the one with the most to learn.

It was expected that at graduation we would be given new challenges and one was already mapped out for me in the promotion to marketing manager. I was therefore surprised to receive a call from Fred Meyer, by now head of Coca-Cola in Southern Africa, offering me the position of general manager of Coca-Cola Bottling Company of Johannesburg. I accepted immediately, as this was truly my dream job. It was also more attractive as a new venture since Coca-Cola had just agreed to purchase the Schweppes business from South African Breweries, along with some of SAB's own brands, a deal I had been involved with right before going to Harvard. My job, therefore, would involve integrating these new operations into Coca-Cola. It would also be a turnaround challenge since Coke's market share in Johannesburg had been slipping over the last year. I quickly called Pamela, who was soon to join me in Boston for the Thanksgiving holiday. What a celebration. I was back in the franchisee side of the business as a bottler, with no regrets whatsoever.

My office was in a factory in an industrial area near the center of Johannesburg. Sitting at my desk, I could hear the bottling lines running. I was now, at age thirty-three, in charge of two factories and seventeen hundred employees. While the head office was only a few miles away, I was running my "own" business. There is, however, a lonely feeling as you close your office door and realize you are the leader, particularly as some former peers, all older than you, now report to you.

Coca-Cola shipped concentrate to our plant in gallon jars and we would use that to make the syrup that would then be mixed with carbonated water and bottled. The ingredients that go into the concentrate are mixed secretly in a few select locations around the world.

I was also, ironically, a Pepsi bottler, as South African Breweries had discontinued its Pepsi franchise. Pepsi sued on antitrust grounds in the U.S. and a deal had been struck that in order to ensure access to the Johannesburg marketplace, we would continue to bottle Pepsi brands.

Among the many challenges I faced as plant manager, there were two urgent ones. The first was the integration of the Schweppes business. Although technically a merger, Coke owned 82 percent of the shares in the new company, and Coke executives held nearly all the key management jobs after the first round of job cuts to eliminate duplicate roles. In the second round I tried to ensure that we kept some of the Schweppes managers, and (in my view) in one or two instances I selected the slightly inferior Schweppes managers to correct what I perceived might be my own Coca-Cola bias. Bad mistake. Only one of them survived beyond a year as the Schweppes cultural fit was so different. We were doing it the Coca-Cola way, not developing—as I would learn to do later in my career—a new culture that would accommodate both sides.

The second urgent move was the implementation of the Sullivan Code, which Coca-Cola executives in Atlanta had agreed to against the wishes of most of the South African management. One objection, a valid one, was that what we were doing was violating South African law, which was, of course, Reverend Sullivan's intent. For example, the Sullivan Code demanded integration of toilets and canteen facilities. Apartheid theoretically meant separate but equal facilities, but in reality it was separate but inferior. The physical part of complying with Sullivan was the easy part—just a small amount of construction was required. However, we faced many challenges.

There were two categories of employees: managers who were paid monthly and nonmanagement who were paid weekly. While all the nonmanagement workers were black, the managers were split 50-50 between white and other races, which included an Asian contingent. The classification laws in South Africa were so complex that on occasion, children in the same family were classified differently based on skin color and the curliness of their hair.

Another challenge was in maintaining the spirit and the letter of the Sullivan Code. At first, we discovered white female workers going across the street to use another company's segregated toilets. I tried with my management team to set an example in the cafeteria by sitting, often creating, mixed-race tables. One day, my head of human resources came to me with the information that the black employees on the serving staff had been bribed to keep certain plates for the exclusive use (and separate washing) of one group. I thought the plates were reserved for white employees only to discover by tracking plates that had been marked with nail polish on the underside that they were exclusively used by the Asian group.

Then there were the visits from the government inspectors who would demand to meet with me to quote in detail the apartheid laws that we had breached and the potential penalties, which included me being jailed. I would agree that the law had been broken and we would shake hands and await the next repeat act. Apartheid was eroding, and the reality was that to arrest and jail a Coca-Cola executive would have created an international incident. There were also cracks in the government's classification of jobs reserved for whites. As this was constantly breached by both foreign and South African companies, the apartheid government would pass new laws effectively legalizing the facts on the ground.

I did what I could to change the racial equation, hiring Coke's first black sales manager in South Africa, Ernest Mchunu. Although Coke had already begun to hire black route salesmen, all the sales managers were white, even those whose territory included the black townships. Ernest and I had worked together in a Johannesburg clothing chain store shortly after I graduated from college. I knew that he had management potential. Coke, after endorsing the Sullivan principles, had hired Ernest as a public relations officer, basically to be the black face of the business. He was trotted out to company functions as a way to show that Coke had black management, and he had an impressive title, but no real power and no one working for him. I thought he was capable of doing more, so I recruited him to be the sales manager in Soweto.

For Ernest, it was a tough call. In the public relations function, he was eating in the best restaurants in Johannesburg and meeting the top Coke executives and visitors when they traveled from Atlanta. Yet the sales manager job would be real work. When he at first declined the offer, I told him, "You are being used, Ernest. Do you want to be the white man's tame black face or do you want a real career? If you don't come and get the experience now, you are never going to be able to get into general management." After talking it over with his wife, he took the job. Unfortunately, after I left South Africa, I was replaced by an old-style plant manager. He and Ernest did not get along and Ernest left to manage Pepsi's operations in Uganda, having gained management experience that made him far more valuable in the beverage industry.

In South Africa, I experienced government price controls for the first time, and saw firsthand the strange effects of intervention in the free-market system.

The South African government had imposed price controls in order to contain inflation. A key component of an effective price control program is maintaining healthy competition in the marketplace. In order to raise prices, a company had to first submit a detailed profit/loss statement to government authorities. Coca-Cola did not favor this system, but strangely, we benefited from it enormously.

There were a number of small soft drink companies which controlled only tiny shares of the market. One was called Goldberg & Zeffert and it had the 7UP franchise in South Africa. Its strategy was to price its soft drinks 15 percent below Coca-Cola's, producing very thin profit margins. As a result, Goldberg & Zeffert was always the first to go to the government seeking price increases.

Coca-Cola's profit margins were quite healthy, however, and each time the government granted a price increase, it enhanced our bottom line even further. However, if the government denied a price increase, small operators such as Goldberg & Zeffert might well go out of business.

The decision before the government bureaucrat was very simple: Does he put the small operator out of business or does he grant the price increase and ensure the continued high level of profitability of the main player? It was an interesting conundrum and illustrates what happens when the natural order of the marketplace is disrupted by government intervention. The effect was that most consumers in South Africa paid more, not less, for their soft drinks. It illustrates why, in my opinion, government price controls rarely work.

I sensed from day one in Johannesburg that mine was a transitional job, and that if it went well, it would launch my career out of Africa onto the world stage. This was confirmed about a year after taking the general manager's job, when I got a call from Ian Wilson, who was now in Atlanta, in charge of Coke in Asia. Wilson had become the consummate Coca-Cola insider, bird hunting with company patriarch Robert W. Woodruff at his South Georgia plantation, Ichauway. Woodruff would send Wilson roses on his birthday, just as he did to other top Coke executives in the inner circle.

"Neville, are you ready yet to work outside South Africa?" Wilson asked me. I told him I wasn't quite ready yet, that I wanted to gain more experience at the bottling plant before moving out. "When you're ready, call me," he replied.

In late 1979, during my annual performance review, I was offered the job as head of all the bottling plants in Southern

Africa, a major promotion. I turned it down. I was now ready to leave South Africa, to gain global experience. I then made the call to Wilson in Atlanta. He circulated the information around the North Avenue tower and in the spring of 1980, I was called to Atlanta. Wilson offered me the job as Coca-Cola's general manager in Australia.

There was one company-owned bottler in Sydney, which would report to me. The other bottlers were franchisees. This was a regional manager's job, but the promise was that within a year, I would be a division president, in charge of Australia, New Zealand, and the surrounding islands, one of only eighteen divisions in the world. I flew from Atlanta to New York to get a visa, and then on to Australia for a briefing on the new position. In that one week, I flew literally around the world, from Johannesburg to Atlanta, Atlanta to New York, New York to Sydney, and then back to Johannesburg.

It was with great sadness that we left South Africa, a country I still love, a country where in many ways, I had become a real adult. Pamela was also sad to be leaving "our" continent after twenty-six years. We still return to Africa yearly and support many NGOs there.

When we moved to Sydney in early 1980, Cara was only two years old. Sydney reminded us, on the surface, of South Africa. In my view, of the five most beautiful cities in the world, Sydney and Cape Town are both on the list. Looking for a house, we had grandiose ideas of water views and being able to go down to the beach every morning for a swim and the like. Yet we found ourselves half a million dollars short of that goal, settling instead for a $200,000 Cape Cod home with a deck and pool on a beautifully wooded lot about ten miles north of the city.

We were still only twenty minutes away from the beach and we would often load a cooler with prawns, oysters, and a bottle of wine and set off to the beach to watch the sunset and have a late swim. We attended the opera, the ballet, horse races, and a ball to raise money for the duck-billed platypus. We made some friends, the closest being Lyn and Mike Hall, and discovered some second and third cousins living in Australia.

While Sydney had great physical beauty, we found it to be a very provincial city and we were never really happy there. It's an international city now, but it wasn't then and I found it difficult to make friends outside the office. There were constant labor strikes that disrupted business as well as day-to-day life. The cost of living was about 10 percent higher than in South Africa, and even more for any service that involved labor, such as gardeners, babysitters, and garbage collection.

My new position was also particularly difficult because of harsh tension between the Coca-Cola Company and the Australian bottlers. The man who ran the bottling plant in Brisbane, Arch Ball, was a rough character, street-smart and tough, but with absolutely no sophistication or culture.

Just before we moved to Australia, a group of Australian bottlers, including Ball, just happened to be visiting Johannesburg. I hosted a dinner for them at our house, which was for sale because we were in the process of moving to Sydney. Ball cornered Pamela and told her, "It would be a bloody mistake for you to sell the house. You'll need it again in six months after the Australian bottlers are finished with Neville." He was serious.

One of the first priorities in a new country is very simply to travel it and visit with the bottlers and the customers. It was also one of the most interesting voyages of discovery as there was no

homogeneity, and each province or city has its own culture defined by its history, location, and climate. Brisbane, the capital
of Queensland, is the brashest of the major Australian cities and
Queensland's history as a sugarcane state gives it a rough edge
only slightly smoothed by the advent of tourism. Ball, the bottler general manager, was a former cane cutter and proud of it,
and displayed a breadth of language and political incorrectness
to match. On my first visit to Brisbane, he hosted a dinner at the
top of the Hilton Hotel in a private room with a wonderful
view. The major customers and wholesalers together with the
owner of the largest tourism business and the owner of the dog
racing track who was Ball's best "mate" were there. Plied with
copious amounts of alcohol and great seafood (yabbies are one of
the world's great crustaceans) they not too gently told me how
they saw the world and their distaste for anything refined, or as
they put it, the world of the "poofters."

In a way it was an evening of survival as I tried to bridge the
gap by discussing sports. In Australia, this worked like a charm
as it was and is the world's most sport-obsessed nation. It's a
reflection of the outdoors lifestyle and the love of life that
makes even the roughest Aussies fun to be with . . . but then I
am a sports "nut" myself.

The party wound up about midnight and I certainly knew
that I'd imbibed too much as I battled with my room key to at
last escape to bed. About five minutes later, there was a knock
on my door and I yelled "wait" as I searched for a towel to wrap
around my naked frame. (Being tall, I found hotel dressing
gowns didn't always provide sufficient coverage.) There at the
door was an attractive and young dark-haired woman in a
miniskirt who greeted me as Neville. I politely asked who she

was and she asked to enter the room. As I hesitated and gathered my thoughts, she said, "Arch (the bottler) sent me and it's all paid for." Now we all know that alcohol weakens inhibition, and I don't claim to be one of the world's innocents, but I did have the good sense to politely say good night and close the door in her face. I had survived a test but I also had Arch's number. Within the month, Mike Hall, one of my great friends throughout my Coke career and my life who was the marketing manager for the Australian division and worked for me, removed two Coke employees for code of conduct violations. They had worked very "well" with Arch. We were never able to prove specifically that they had accepted the bribe of a prostitute, but they had broken company policy in other ways by doing favors for the bottler.

In the summer of 1980, I flew to Tokyo to make my first business plan presentation on Australia to Ian Wilson, who was now a company vice chairman. He had good news: He was about to be named Chairman and CEO of the Coca-Cola Company, replacing Paul Austin, who was retiring. Ian invited me to have a congratulatory drink with him later that night in his hotel suite. His executive assistant, Peter George, met me at the door. He and Ian clearly had been drinking. It turned out that Ian had just received a call from Atlanta informing him that the plans had changed. Roberto Goizueta, a Cuban who had defected to the United States in 1961 while on vacation in Miami, would be the new CEO and Chairman. I was sitting with an embittered Ian in his hotel room, his career at Coke over, all the stories and all the bile coming out. Austin had recommended Ian for the job and even held a celebratory dinner, wives included. Yet Robert W. Woodruff had overruled Austin in favor of Goizueta.

Ian told me Woodruff did not want a South African to head the company. In 1980, international opposition to apartheid was rapidly building.

In 1994 a still embittered Ian tried to launch a Pepsi franchise in South Africa after the fall of apartheid. The venture failed miserably. In 2001 Ian was sentenced to more than two years in prison after pleading guilty in the U.S. to securities fraud for misrepresenting the financial statements of Aurora Foods, a company he founded.

After that awkward night in Tokyo, I returned to Sydney somewhat unsettled about my future. It had been Ian who engineered my move to Australia and had promised me the division president's job, and he was now leaving the company.

In early 1981, Sam Ayoub, an Egyptian who had succeeded Wilson as head of Asia, flew down to Sydney for a visit and we had dinner at the American Club. My boss in Australia, Robert Patterson, the division manager whose job I was supposed to assume within a year, was notorious as one who always had to retire early in the evening, demanding that company dinners end no later than nine o'clock. Just to annoy Patterson, Ayoub suggested we play the slot machines after dinner. Patterson declined but Sam and I walked over to try our luck. As we were standing there pulling the handles, Ayoub said, "You know the plan for you taking over from Robert, that's still there. I'm taking him back to Atlanta. You're going to be the division president." Someone new had come in, taken a good hard look at the business, and decided that Ian's plan was sound. I was greatly relieved.

A few weeks later, Robert Patterson and I were visiting a bottler in Newcastle when Sam phoned. It was a Tuesday and he wanted me to be in Manila by Thursday to spend a week in the Philippines with John Hunter, the region manager, who was later to be one of the two principal operating officers of the Coca-Cola Company and clearly President Don Keough's choice to be next CEO and Chairman. I told Robert that Sam wanted me in Manila on Thursday.

"What's that about?" Robert asked.

"I don't know, something about a joint venture," I replied.

"Don't go," Robert said, although he clearly realized that I had to make the trip. "That's a crazy deal they're putting together."

I hurried back to Sydney and was soon off on a plane to Manila. When we arrived at the scruffy airport, John Hunter was waiting for me at the bottom of the steps of the plane.

Coca-Cola's plans for me had changed dramatically and Hunter's career and mine were to become happily intertwined.

Three

CONQUERING PEPSI IN THE PHILIPPINES

oca-Cola was losing the Philippines. And failure there might have marked the beginning of the end of the company's global business.

In 1981, the Philippines was the tenth largest soft drink market in the world, but Pepsi had a 2 to 1 market lead (double that in the capital city of Manila). The Coke bottler, owned by the famous beer maker San Miguel Corporation, was losing $5 million a year. It warned that it could no longer sustain the losses and threatened to exit the bottling business unless Coca-Cola shared the burden.

At Coke headquarters in Atlanta, international markets were falling into disfavor as the U.S. dollar soared, which hurt overseas profits. John Collins, Coke's new chief financial officer, made strong statements that the company was too exposed to international markets and that the goal was to increase the U.S. share of profits to more than 50 percent through acquisitions.

This led to the purchase of Columbia Pictures and investments in the wine business.

John Hunter, then head of Coca-Cola in the Philippines and later to become head of Coca-Cola International, was tenacious in convincing upper management that it would be disastrous for Coca-Cola to cede a Top Ten overseas market. His view was backed by the company's new president, Don Keough, and other top executives including Sam Ayoub, who had succeeded Wilson as head of Asia.

Hunter was the father of the deal. He worked out an agreement with members of the Sorianos family, who were major stockholders for decades, to sell Coca-Cola 30 percent of the bottling operation for $30 million. That doesn't seem like much money now—in 2010 Coke announced plans to spend $1 billion in the Philippines over the next five years—but at the time it was Coke's largest single foreign investment.

Roberto Goizueta took the proposal to the board of directors, his first major decision as CEO and Chairman. At that time, it was very much a board of Southern gentlemen, many of an advanced age. It was not unusual, as I was to experience firsthand eighteen months later, for board members to nod off during meetings. I don't know how much trouble Roberto had convincing the board to invest in a country run by Ferdinand Marcos, a dictator who was entering the end of his reign, where future stability was questionable. Roberto did tell me later that in order to avoid undermining him, a few board members had abstained rather than vote against the proposal.

Hunter convinced the Sorianos that the new joint venture needed to have an experienced Coca-Cola bottling executive as its president and controller. I was named the first president of the joint venture, in part because of my experience with two Coke bottlers in Africa.

My executive assistant was from San Miguel, a man named Romy Dalandan, who would show me the ropes but was also clearly watching me and reporting back to the 70 percent shareholders. One of my main challenges, therefore, was to prove that I was independent of both Coke and the Sorianos and that I was running the company for the benefit of both groups of shareholders without being adversarial to either side. This was complicated to a degree since we were disengaging from central San Miguel services including sensitive areas such as purchasing.

From day one, the Philippines was not expected to be an easy assignment. Coke had attempted a turnaround there before and failed. One apparent advantage for Pepsi was that its bottler in the Philippines was wholly owned by the parent company. So for Pepsi, any return on investment from higher bottler profits went entirely back to headquarters. Conversely, Coke would have to share a large portion of its gains with the Sorianos.

Hunter's view was that over time, the franchise model could work well in the Philippines and I fully agreed with him. Coke's profit margins on the sale of concentrate are higher than the margins the bottler makes on its operations, justified by the power of the brand. Bottling can be an excellent business if well run. The lower profit margins for the bottlers force them to operate more efficiently. At the same time, Coke had to live up to its end of the bargain by building the brand.

Conversely, the Pepsi structure in the Philippines did not produce the intense focus needed for running successful bottling operations in the long term, as they would soon discover.

For the time being, however, Pepsi was outselling us 4 to 1 in some areas of the country, including Manila, not just with Pepsi but with Mountain Dew, Mirinda Orange, and 7UP. The Philippines was Pepsi's number two market in the world and was featured in a 1981 annual report as a prime example of how to beat Coke.

This was a risky venture and clearly a number of people had much to lose, including me. I was told by many people inside the company that failure was almost certain.

Ian Wilson, who had been so close to being chairman and had given me my Australia opportunity, was sure this was a way of pushing me out the door for being his prodigy. I didn't accept that since I knew I had strong support not only from Goizueta, but from Keough and Ayoub. Goizueta, in his first meeting with me after I took the job, assured me that he was putting his own reputation on the line as well as Hunter's. However, as the saying goes, success has many fathers and failure is an orphan. I knew the risk, but as ever, the challenge excited me. Also, I was young enough to take the risk and prove, not in the least to myself, that I could lead a large company in a complex environment.

If I failed, I could either go back out on my own or find another opportunity. The other incentive was a $200,000 tax-free bonus for signing up for five years, a fortune to me in those days, but also an indication that others before me had turned down the job offer.

I have a belief system that when the Good Lord created the world, he created Coke number one and Pepsi number two. The Philippines was a terrible aberration, one of only a handful of markets in the world where Coke trailed Pepsi. It was fixable. That wasn't just my blind faith, despite the fact that the eighteen Coke bottling plants were run down and some should have been closed. The index measuring the quality of Coke plants in the country was 29 on a scale of 100. It was about the same as the market share against Pepsi.

Then I looked at Pepsi and saw they weren't a great deal better in terms of quality and execution. They were just more aggressive in the marketplace, but aggressive without discipline.

However, when I took Pamela to Manila for three days to look over the place, my chance to lead the turnaround almost fell apart. Riding into Manila from the airport, Pamela was appalled at the country's abject poverty. The road, unfortunately, ran adjacent to a horrible slum. We were both from Africa, but this was far worse than anything in Africa at the time. In the hot tropical climate, the garbage and the filth was starting to emit a foul odor.

"Darling, I don't think I can do this," Pamela told me before we reached the hotel. I realized we had a problem and understood her reluctance, but convinced her that we should complete the three-day trip and then decide.

She felt better as we entered Makati, the Manila business district, and checked into the Peninsula Hotel and later when we had dinner in the Champagne Room of the old Manila Hotel, where General Douglas MacArthur had lived when the Japanese attacked in 1941. Pamela agreed to give the Philippines a try and we were soon on our way.

The company provided us with a first-class house complete with a swimming pool, three maids, a driver, a gardener, and two security guards. Even by African standards, this was almost a surplus of servants. Our daughter, Cara, had her own nanny, or "yaya." We added another family member as well, Sebastian, a basset hound. The friendliness of the people and our ease at making friends soon meant that as a family we settled in rapidly. The only security problem we had was when one of our guards shot himself in the foot while playing with his gun.

The Philippines consists of about 7,100 islands, many of them uninhabited. In a typical year, many regions receive 100 inches of rain. When it rains, it pours, as Manila is in the typhoon belt.

The country has an interesting cultural mix of former Malay tribal structure influenced by more than two hundred years of Spanish rule and more than forty years of U.S. control. English is widely spoken and literacy is relatively high. In the 1980s, some predicted that the Philippines, which then had 50 million people, could be the next Japan, an economic giant. For a variety of reasons, most related to the Philippine political process, that has not materialized, although the country still has enormous potential. One of the striking features of the Philippines is how similar it is to Mexico in architecture and design. Spain administered the islands out of Acapulco. The marketplace in old Acapulco where fish and vegetables are sold looks remarkably like a standard one in Manila.

Despite such similarities, the influence of the United States on the Philippines is difficult to ignore. A number of the television programs and newspapers are in English and most Filipinos have relatives living in the U.S. This veneer of U.S. culture, mixed with a laissez-faire, Spanish-Malay way of living, creates a sort of organized chaos, a bubbling, cheerful society where people appear to be generally happy, even those who are poor. Obviously, poverty takes its toll in many ways, but enjoying oneself is at the center of many Filipino's lives. *Merienda*, big daily rituals revolving around food, with snack breaks during the morning and afternoon, stop work in the office and are an important part of the culture, one that is not to be interfered with.

The Catholic Church is strong in the Philippines and its voice is heard in all moral and political debates. Church attendance and the observation of various church festivals are major events. Each year at Easter, men are actually hung on crosses and flagellated on the streets. Yet, as in any society, in the Philippines there is a dichotomy.

In every town and particularly evident in Manila are "short-term" hotels—very profitable businesses—where normal stays are for three hours. They advertise heavily, particularly around Valentine's Day. After checking in, you are directed to a vacant garage and the door is closed behind you. Your room is directly above the garage and fairly garish with plenty of mirrors. Food and drink are available as room service. How do I know all of this? Well, Pamela and I decided to sample one as part of a desire to "explore," which proved of great interest when I relayed the story one evening at a friend's dinner party, although there were a few concerned faces around the table.

An expat is able to live to a degree within Philippine society. In Japan, you go to a formal business event but you very rarely go to someone's home. In the Philippines, it is not unusual to be invited to someone's home. There is a level of integration between expats and Filipinos that I have not seen anywhere else in Asia.

When we first arrived, President Marcos had just been re-elected to a new six-year term and the political situation appeared to be stable, although conditions would deteriorate steadily during our time there. George Bush, then vice president under Ronald Reagan, honored Marcos with a state visit, prompting protests from the opposition.

For the first time, I had my own major company to run, but it was in an exotic country of which I knew little. For any global company, there is no more important task than fully understanding the culture of the country where you are operating. This lesson was ingrained in me in the Philippines.

Before arriving, I read as much as I could about Filipino culture, something I had failed to do when we moved to Australia, making the incorrect assumption that it would be like South Africa. In the Philippines, family allegiance is extremely strong. Allegiance to your classmates, either from the military or in school, is actually greater than any allegiance people would have for their employer.

The cultural traits include *Utang na loob,* which means obligation. If I do you a favor, you have to return the favor some time in the future. *Pakikisama* means getting along, avoiding confrontation when first meeting someone. Filipinos also tend to search for common lineage with others all the way to a third cousin, and seem to have an encyclopedic knowledge of their detailed family trees.

In Filipino culture, "yes" often means "I hear you," not "I agree with you." Ensuring you have agreement is therefore much more complex. The worst thing to do is get annoyed and say, "You agreed to do this." In your view, they did. In their view, they didn't. In other words, you're in *their* culture and you need to understand the way *their* culture works. You can't impose your culture on them. Of course you maintain your standards and your values. That's a different issue. Yet at the same time, you have to bend with the cultural wind if you're going to be able to work in any country and find ways to achieve your goals within this frame.

Once in the Philippines, I realized immediately that I needed to hire a Filipino manager, someone who knew the business but could also be a cultural interpreter. John Hunter, who had designed the five-year plan, had already come to that same conclusion and had a recommendation. That man turned out to be Jesus Celdran, nicknamed King King or King^2.

I met him over lunch at the Manila Polo Club. Physically, the two of us didn't match at all. King is five foot six and I'm about a foot taller. Eventually our nickname became Mutt and Jeff. We were joined at the hip—well, we couldn't have been because of the height difference—but metaphorically, we were.

With King King our basic team was complete. In addition to him and myself was Tony Eames, an Australian transferred from Atlanta to be manager of Coca-Cola in the Philippines. He'd replaced John Hunter, who had been promoted to Hong Kong. Tony and I were in our thirties, King King about twenty years older. We traveled the length and breadth of that country together. King King in particular was absolutely crucial to my success. He was the one who was able to understand what I was trying to do strategically. He was able to say, "Well, I like your idea but here's why it doesn't work in the Philippines," and even more important, he'd explain how we could make it work.

For example, once we were discussing sales incentives. We had a business of 10,500 employees. My thinking was that we could leverage the sales incentives. Instead of giving employees a $200 bonus, we could actually give them a refrigerator that was worth $400 because we could buy the appliances at cost from the manufacturer. We'd be giving them double the value of prizes for the same cost, and this would also act as a family incentive.

"No boss, that doesn't work," King King told me. He explained that when a salesman wins a $200 bonus, it goes into his back pocket. It's his play money, unlike his salary, which he takes home and gives to his wife. In the Philippines, the woman manages the family and handles the money and basically gives an allowance to the husband. My plan would not have worked culturally. Logic does not always prevail.

In one of my first meetings with senior management, I addressed another sensitive cultural issue, expat salaries, which were much higher than those of the Filipino execs. I explained to my Filipino direct reports that this was necessary to attract foreign talent and that I myself had been paid less than an American in South Africa, who ran the much smaller bottling plant in Durban. While I was not particularly pleased about that, I understood he could not be paid on the local pay scale.

"I've brought these people in. I think we need that injection of new talent," I told the Filipino managers. "At the end of the month, you are going to think about what they walk away with and what you walk away with for equal effort and if you disagree with that, you shouldn't be part of the team. I don't want there to be a burning resentment about higher expat salaries and benefits around that element. Absent that one difference, we're not going to be the expats in one corner, the Filipinos in another. We are one team." I meant that and lived by it, as did the three expats I had brought in.

Pepsi, in a later reaction to Coke's resurgence in the Philippines, brought in a new team of expats. They committed the sin that I was avoiding. The expats sat around at the Manila Polo Club, drank beer, and complained about the Filipinos being lazy. That is what happens when management is disconnected from society. It leads to alienation all around and a lack of understanding of the market and the customers.

From day one in the Philippines, I began the process of modernizing the bottling plants and energizing the sales force. No one was more important in this process than Tony Eames, the region manager of the Coca-Cola Company. He had no ego when it came to sharing decision-making on advertising, which was normally the purview of the Coca-Cola Company. The advertising campaign from headquarters at the time was "Have a Coke and a Smile." With Pepsi outselling us 4 to 1 in Manila, I thought we needed a stronger message. Also, Pepsi had singer Michael Jackson, who was extremely popular in the Philippines, in its ads. So we developed our own commercials, using Filipino stars, advertising both the Coca-Cola brand and featuring our new packaging. It could have been interpreted as a violation of the company rules since all brand advertising had to come through Atlanta. Yet Tony allowed us to do this, arguing that it was packaging advertising, which was exempted. Also, with only one bottler in the Philippines, it made more sense to collaborate with us during our early stage of storyboard development. He was right. I reciprocated by allowing him to give his input on manufacturing issues, which were normally reserved only for bottlers. It was a great lesson on how the franchise system should and could work.

Joe Brand from Coca-Cola Company joined my team as head of quality control to ensure that the bottling plants met global standards. Coke insisted that Joe report directly to me and not to Ramon Abola, the Filipino technical head. I considered this a major mistake as it would undermine Ramon and send a signal to the organization that expats were special. Joe, to his credit, saw this, and agreed to report to Ramon. This reinforced that we were a single team even though Joe earned more money than his boss. Joe never faltered and within three years, quality scores for Coke plants in the Philippines were higher than the world average.

When I interviewed Joe for the job, I was in the Makati Medical Center, with a drip in my arm, weak and emaciated, having lost ten pounds from a bout with typhoid fever and a recurrence of the malaria I had as a child in Africa. I looked like a skeleton. Such was life on the road.

Both before and after my recovery, King King, Tony, and I worked almost every weekend, hopping from one island to the other.

During World War II, King King had served with guerilla forces as an intelligence officer behind Japanese lines under the command of Colonel Wendell Fertig, an American who stayed behind in the Philippines after General MacArthur escaped to Australia.

"We were constantly moving from one camp to another, always in fear for our lives, trying to keep one step ahead of the Japanese," King King recalled in an interview for this book.

King King had great credibility in Mindanao as a war hero, and a facility for languages in this, the most multicultural island in the Philippines. As an interesting aside, former Coke CEO Paul Austin also served behind enemy lines with Filipino guerillas during World War II, obtaining information for U.S. Navy PT boat operations.

When I arrived in the Philippines, Mindanao was still an island of extreme conflict, with two insurgencies underway. The first was led by the communist New People's Army and the second by the Moro Liberation Front. Both groups controlled large sections in the rural areas of the island. And yet, Mindanao was Coke's strongest market.

The conflict with the MLF, which sought independence for Muslim areas, continues even to this day, and the U.S. military is very involved in an advisory capacity.

When King King and I traveled to areas of the Philippines where Muslim influence was strong, we were always accompanied by guards toting their firearms. Often they were positioned outside my bedroom door, even following me to the men's room.

On one isolated island, a couple who had paddled over in a dugout canoe was terrified when we landed in a helicopter. It was almost as if we had stepped back in time a thousand years, as they were members of a remote indigenous tribe. They had no idea of date or time or the peso value of the fish they were catching. We offered them Coke and San Miguel beer, neither of which they had ever tasted. They hated and literally spat out the beer, but loved the Coca-Cola. We had two more satisfied customers.

Appealing to the country's militaristic fascination, King King, Tony Eames, and I created a sales team called the "Tiger Force" with the theme song "Eye of the Tiger," from the movie *Rocky*. To this day, when I hear that song, I'm energized by it. I feel all over again the thrill of the fight.

On Saturdays and Sundays, we would hold sales rallies, with music, good food, San Miguel beer, and theatrics. Once, King

King, Tony, and I dressed as Filipino generals. I would sometimes smash a Pepsi bottle against the wall of a bottling plant, revving up the troops. In one town, the local bottling manager, who was friends with the military officers there, arranged for us to ride to the rally on a tank. This was business war and the enemy was dressed in blue.

Hundreds of route salesmen attended our rallies around the country. They worked six days a week in the tropical heat, driving from one tiny shop to the other, unloading heavy crates of Coke, making sure that the Coca-Cola signage was properly placed (so that it would be more prominent than Pepsi's) and that the coolers were working properly, all the while pitching the store owner to buy new products such as Mello Yello.

When we launched Mello Yello, billed as "the world's fastest soft drink," I would lead the salesmen in calisthenics—doing pushups on the stage—then we'd run around the plant together. It was all about creating energy and drive, and not something I had learned at Harvard Business School.

Many people think the power of Coca-Cola is the strength of the brand. Yet, it's the route salesman who is the unsung hero, the one who does the real heavy lifting, literally and figuratively. Those were the people we tried to motivate. And quickly, we saw the difference in the marketplace. Regularly, we'd go out and tour the sari-saris, as the small shops were called. "Don't expect what you can't inspect" was my motto. Some of the shops were literally tin-roofed shacks and at six foot five, I had to stoop to get through the front doors, not always successfully. Yet we began to see that Coke was gaining more prominence as our signs and products became much more visible. When I toured the bottling plants across the country, there was typically a big lunch and a scripted tour, the factory spruced up for my visit. I made a point of breaking off from the official tour and inspecting the employee bathrooms and locker rooms. If they were not kept clean, it was a sign that the company did not really care about the employees. Workers were sometimes shocked to see me, the president of the company, touring their bathrooms, which were often filthy. It sent a message, from the top, that employees mattered and that quality meant quality in *everything* we did. Everything communicates a message. For example, I would rather have no sign than an old, faded sign.

One of the strategy development methods I have used on occasion is to be sure that we're looking at our business through the lens of our competitor. In Manila, I took the upper management team to a strategy session at the Intercontinental Hotel. They entered a room which was decorated with Pepsi posters. There was ice-cold Pepsi for them to drink, no Coke, and I had Pepsi T-shirts for them to wear. They were obviously shocked. Then I conducted an all-day session designed to detect the weaknesses in the Coca-Cola system and develop a strategy to retain our leadership over Pepsi. During such a session, it takes about an hour for people to get comfortable, but eventually things fall into place and workers get a thoroughly honest assessment of their own flaws and strengths. Interpreting the data over the following days clearly helps to build better business strategies. It's amazing the brutal honesty that comes from these sessions, and how hidden flaws that most people are naturally reluctant to admit to are uncovered. Goizueta, the Coca-Cola CEO and chairman, helped our cause, flying in for a visit to Manila. It was interesting to see Roberto, a Cuban, in his Spanish mode. The Sorianos were Spanish Filipinos and still had roots in Spain and they bonded with Goizueta completely.

We had a lunch that went on and on and afterward, the Sorianos and Goizueta disappeared to carry on drinking. It was pretty clear in the evening that they had a very good session. At a major evening party, Roberto, the Sorianos, and yours truly did the *tinikling,* a Filipino dance in which two women hold bamboo poles and slide them together on the ground to the rhythm of the music. The dancer has to jump out before getting his feet caught between the poles. I had never seen Roberto like that. He was an extremely disciplined man but here he was immersed in the Spanish fun culture.

Don Keough, president of Coke, later paid a visit with John Georgas, head of Coke's international sales. At a sales rally, I had Don and John dressed in Tiger Force T-shirts as I led employees in motivational chants. "We could have led a revolution with that crowd, that day," Don later said.

In the Philippines, my ability as a public speaker started to improve. I could rally people. I learned how to control an audience. It was a major turning point for me. Visiting the Philippines, Goizueta and Keough saw me in a totally different light. I sensed that I was starting to get on their radar screen as the turnaround progressed, and I was later invited to address a global meeting and to speak to the company board of directors in Atlanta.

Around this same time, I met President Marcos for the first time and noticed that he did not appear healthy. His face was puffy, an indication of what would later be diagnosed as lupus. Both his health and political empire were in rapid decline. That was unsettling in the long term, but in the short term, we did not let that interfere with our campaign to defeat Pepsi.

At the end of the first twelve months, Coca-Cola was close to regaining the lead in market share, led by the energized sales force and by new products such as Mello Yello. Coca-Cola had also purchased a brand from San Miguel called Royal Tru-Orange, which did much better than Pepsi's Mirinda brand. New packaging was the major contributor to a growth surge.

Pepsi had been selling a 12-oz bottle for the same price as an 8-oz drink, which I was sure was not sustainable even with cross subsidies from the concentrate profits. San Miguel, which had been operating at a loss, had lacked sufficient capital to convert to 12-oz bottles but the Coke investment made that possible. Still, San Miguel's glass manufacturing capacity was limited and importing glass was too expensive.

The original plan had been to eliminate all the 8-oz bottles, as Pepsi had done, and go strictly to 12-oz. I decided to keep the 8 oz bottle, realizing there was a need for a lower-cost drink in the market and that Pepsi could not continue to sell the 12-oz at the current price as inflation was deteriorating their profit margin. Keeping the 8-oz bottle also saved us money because it lowered the number of new 12-oz bottles we had to produce. It also meant fewer new crates. At the time, we were shifting from wooden crates—which rotted easily in the tropical climate—to plastic ones. Much more important, keeping 8-oz bottles meant that we could accelerate by at least a year the national rollout of the new 12-oz bottle as manufacturing capacity for new bottles was limited and therefore constrained our aggressive rollout.

It is hard to imagine now, in the world of aluminum cans and plastic bottles, how important returnable glass bottles were in those days. A large portion of a bottler's assets were tied up in glass. That's why companies charged deposits on bottles, to ensure that customers returned them for reuse instead of throwing them away.

One of the first things I noted upon arriving in the Philippines was that there was a game going on between Pepsi and Coke. Both companies were "stealing" each other's bottles in an attempt to drain the competitor's assets by forcing them to purchase more glass. Both companies had mounds of their opponent's bottles stacked in vast fields. And because of the damp tropical climate, weeds soon covered the fields and rainwater—followed soon after by algae—filled the bottles. I have seen companies steal one another's bottles in other parts of the world, but the extent of it in the Philippines was unbelievable. Immediately I ordered the practice stopped on our end, prompting Pepsi forces to label King King, Tony Eames, and me the Boy Scouts. Quietly they began to reduce the level at which they removed our bottles.

As we tried to figure out how Pepsi was making a profit despite the *low* prices they were charging in the marketplace for *larger* bottles, we began to suspect it might have something to do with the accounting for bottle deposits.

The deposits were normally set by agreement between the two companies. It was not price fixing but an agreement on the value of an asset: the bottle. Both Coke and Pepsi had been increasing their deposits to the point where they were closing in on the full value of the bottle. Normally, the deposit was far less than the full value. The difference between the deposit and the full value of the bottle was supposed to be placed on a company's balance sheet as a cost—amortized over the life of the bottle—and a debit against profits. For example, if a bottle cost the company 50 cents but the retailer had paid a deposit of only 10 cents, then the company had experienced, effectively, a loss of

40 cents that it would list as a debit on its balance sheet, spreading that loss over the anticipated life of the bottle.

I had agreed to one deposit increase with Pepsi just after I arrived in the Philippines because with inflation, I was worried that the deposit was not high enough to motivate consumers to return the bottles. Pepsi later came back with a proposal to raise the deposit price *above* the value of the bottles. That's when the penny dropped. Pepsi was using the deposit increases to fuel its profits and those profits were funding the battle with Coca-Cola. When I refused another deposit increase, the game was over and Pepsi's false profits evaporated. What I had not realized was that every time the deposit price increased, Pepsi's local management was writing up the value of their bottles, including the redundant ones sitting in the fields, and they were showing their gains as an operating profit. Pepsi was forced to take an $85 million charge to profits, some of this related to Mexico, where a similar practice was being undertaken. In the aftermath, with completely new management, the company decided to lower its deposit, which instantly took money out of the pockets of the dealers who held those bottles in their stores. If a dealer had paid a 50 cent deposit for the bottle, he could redeem it now for only 25 cents. This created an angry network of retailers.

In order to stay competitive, we were forced to match Pepsi's deposit decrease. Otherwise, when a dealer wanted to expand his inventory, Pepsi would have a cost advantage because of the lower deposit and therefore lower cash outlay the dealer would pay. In order to keep our retailers happy, we decided to pay them the old, higher deposit for the bottles they already had in stock. So if they paid a 50 cent deposit, they could return the bottle for 50 cents, not the new, lower rate. This amounted to a

$1 million loss for our company. That was a large sum, since at that time we were making only $2 million a year in profit. The decision, however, shifted the market psychology further against Pepsi, which lost its integrity with the dealers. With the sales growth that followed our decision, we recouped the $1 million within a year. I credit our Filipino treasurer, Chito Gonsalves, for pushing me to make this decision based on the values we shared. It was a victory for integrity.

Another big mistake made by Pepsi was failing to attack Coke's market share on the island of Mindanao. Since Coke had a strong market lead in Mindanao, we could charge higher prices. Those profits were used to combat Pepsi in Manila, where Coke was outsold 4 to 1. Since Pepsi had such a big lead in Manila, it had to spend four dollars to match every dollar we invested in the capital city. If Pepsi had applied the same strategy against Coke in Mindanao, it would have strangled our top profit center. For some reason, Pepsi never seriously challenged us in Mindanao, a major strategic mistake.

And so, in 1983, Coke took the lead in the Philippines, one of the fastest turnarounds in a major market in the company's history. At the same time, the Marcos regime was looking shakier by the day, with growing protests and political upheaval. I walked through one protest in the financial district of Makati and saw a typewriter nearly hit the mayor of Manila, the typewriter having descended from a window seventeen floors above to the stage where the mayor was speaking.

The unrest had a chilling effect on foreign investment in the Philippines. Yet Coke continued to gain over Pepsi and our profits increased steadily. We built a new bottling plant in Manila and undertook massive upgrades at four other plants. The quality of our existing plants soon rose from a score of 29 to above 90, and equaled world averages by 1985.

Meanwhile, our family life was also undergoing some changes. Cara transferred from a Montessori school to the British School in Manila, trading her Philippine accent for a British one.

We spent many weekends at some of the beautiful beach resorts in the Philippines, in particular Maya Maya with its nipa palm huts, bamboo floors, and magnificent view of the beautiful South China Sea. With profits made on a "bet" on yen appreciation against the dollar, we bought a speedboat which allowed us to explore the coast and also gave me great pleasure as I developed my water-skiing skills.

Then we used the $200,000 bonus for accepting the Philippines job to buy our first house in France, taking advantage of the depressed French economy and weak franc, which was due in part to the then socialist government, which cohabitated with the communists. Our farmhouse was built in the eighteenth century, with stonewalls a foot thick that backed up to a giant forest. Although we loved the Philippines, we felt like we needed a base in Western culture, a place to return for three or four weeks each summer to unwind after countless fifteen-hour workdays in Manila.

One of the more taxing tasks that I had during my time in the Philippines was to be a judge—along with the U.S. consul general and others who were believed to have a fine eye for the female figure—in the Miss Philippines contest. The consul general and I had appeared on *Two for the Road*, a live television talk show hosted by journalist Elvira Manahan. The topic was the Miss Philippines contest and what we thought about Filipino women. The show proved to be very popular and a year later we were invited to appear again. We agreed, but insisted that we sit in the audience and not appear as guests. Yet I was in for a surprise. On this live show, Elvira announced a surprise segment, approached us in the bleachers, introduced me, and posed this question: "You're so tall. How do you manage with women?" It was live television and I had to say something, so I managed to deflect the question by replying, "My wife is five foot eleven. And therefore there isn't really a big height difference whatsoever." She wasn't going to buy that one. "No, no," she said. "With us Filipinos?"

I sometimes get myself in trouble by being too quick-witted and flippant and this was one of those occasions. "It's all a matter of perspective," I said with a big smile on my face. "You are judging in the vertical plane. In the horizontal plane, it's no problem at all."

The next day my phone rang! Some people thought the episode was extremely humorous, but others berated me for overstepping a line in terms of what I should be saying as president of the Coca-Cola bottler in the Philippines. I learned a lesson from that incident and became a lot more disciplined as far as what I said in public.

One of our strangest encounters during our time in the Philippines was watching a demonstration of "psychic surgery." This was practiced widely in the Philippines and also Brazil.

Pamela and I were attending a meeting of the Young President's Club, an organization for corporate presidents under the age of forty, at a Manila hotel. The psychic surgery demonstration was offered as part of the program's entertainment.

We gathered in a hotel room with dim lights, kept back a safe distance from the "surgeon." A woman who was a member of our group and a cancer patient lay on a bed. The "surgeon" performed with his hands only, starting by rubbing the woman's stomach. She was conscious the entire time and in no visible pain. After a few minutes the doctor could be seen—using only his hands and no instrument—pulling blood and tissue out of the woman, which he dumped into a bucket. The woman, her cancerous growth allegedly removed, had no scar but only a red stomach from the surgeon's rubbing. It's typical magician stuff, although we've heard some people endorse it and say that they felt relief from their ailments after the encounter. I tend to think it's a classic case of mind over matter, the power of the mind to bring about a cure.

One of the people with us when we witnessed the surgery actually stole a bloodstained towel which had been used during the operation on his wife. He brought it back to the United States and had it tested. The stain was identified as human blood, but was too old to determine whether it matched the woman's blood type. Sadly, her cancer was not cured.

Another interesting encounter in a Manila hotel involved First Lady Imelda Marcos and the Playboy Club. And no, it did not have anything to do with shoes. It was during the visit by Don Keough and John Georgas in 1985.

Danding Cojuangco, a Marcos associate, had gained control of San Miguel, in effect pushing out the Soriano family. In a meeting at the San Miguel offices, Cojuangco had offered to attend a bottler dinner and awards ceremony that evening.

This being the Philippines, Cojuangco arrived an hour late, escorted by his security team. Coke had security around

Keough, the company president. Members of the two security teams were eyeing one another nervously, since they were all carrying weapons. We managed to get on with the evening, when all of a sudden Cojuangco left to take a phone call. It was Imelda, inviting us to the Presidential Palace. We declined, saying we were occupied with the awards dinner. So Imelda decided to join us at the hotel, arriving a short while later, her security team in tow. Now we had three security teams operating independently.

We had a separate room set aside to meet with the first lady, and Imelda immediately charmed everyone, including my wife, Pamela, and the wives of Keough and Georgas. It was a typical modern hotel meeting room, lacking in ambience. Yet suddenly, with the arrival of Imelda, the room was electrified.

First she made an upbeat speech about the Philippines and her husband's future, even though he was ill and only a year away from losing power. Imelda then proposed a toast to the business partnership, mixing San Miguel beer and Coke, half and half. We reluctantly followed her lead, mixing the same unsavory drink and spoiling good beer and great Coca-Cola. It was a clear demonstration of the first lady's political savvy.

After the dinner, we were to go upstairs to the Playboy Club for a show. "I'll join you," Imelda said enthusiastically, when she learned that the live show would feature the Filipino stars Pops Fernandez and Martin Nievera, both of whom had appeared in Coca-Cola commercials. The problem was that I had arranged for a group of young women to be there as dancing partners—just dancing partners—for the sales execs after the departure of key guests. Fearing that the women's presence might be misinterpreted, I had to make sure the dancers were kept out of the

Playboy Club while Imelda was there. Meanwhile, we progressed upstairs. Somewhere, I have a picture of Keough and Imelda walking up the stairs and a Playboy Bunny standing behind them.

A few minutes later, with three security teams in place—Coke's, San Miguel's, and Imelda's—someone dropped a metal chair on the parquet dance floor. I saw the security guys reaching for guns. Imagine a shootout involving the president of Coke, the head of San Miguel, and the first lady of the Philippines. The end of my career flashed in front of my eyes. It took a few seconds—it seemed like thirty minutes to me at the time—for the security teams to realize it was only a chair and to put down their weapons. It was a very scary moment.

After the entertainment, Imelda was still raring to go. It was midnight and I had promised Don Keough an early evening since he had a 6 A.M. flight. "Let's go and have some coffee," Imelda said. I suggested we go back downstairs to the hotel room where we had eaten dinner. An agitated San Miguel executive blocked the door. "No, no, you can't go in there," he told us. It was the room where the dancing girls were still being closeted, waiting to join the festivities with our sales staff after our departure. Another potential career-ending moment missed!

We retired instead to the hotel restaurant, talking until 2 A.M., Imelda entertaining us with stories of her husband's greatness and how the Filipinos loved their first lady. Modesty was not her strong suit.

Business continued to thrive in the Philippines. It was there that I first started paying attention to Coke's multiplier effect on the local economy. In the smaller stores, Coke represented 20 percent of the total business. When you consider the thousands of Coke employees, store owners, and other vendors, the company had a massive effect on the Filipino economy, doing much to provide employment and help alleviate poverty, an effect that bolstered my belief in the power of capitalism.

Toward the end of my time in the Philippines, Pepsi invited me to breakfast with the company's head of international business. I've always believed that there is absolutely no harm in meeting with the competition provided there are no illegal discussions. Such meetings provide a chance to talk about industry issues and also help one get a good feel for the competition's level of confidence on individual issues. And they are good for *both* sides, which I knew.

The meeting, however, turned out to be different from what I thought it would be. I was offered ownership of 10 percent of the Pepsi bottling franchise in Cape Town if I would sign a management contract for three years to try and resuscitate the business, which had been severely weakened by the Forbes family, owners of the Coke bottler there. I turned Pepsi down on the spot. I was too loyal to Coke. Secondly, I have a dictum, "Don't sell something you don't believe in," which is why I have over my career rejected four offers from cigarette manufacturers. Finally, if I suddenly appeared in Cape Town to run the bottling franchise, Coke would do absolutely everything it could to make me fail. So not only was it something I was unwilling to do, it was something I would have been crazy to even attempt.

In 1985, after four years in the Philippines, I was offered the chance to move to West Germany and head Coke in central Europe. Although San Miguel execs did not want me to leave, and I had a year left on my contract, Don Keough convinced them to let me go. I was off to a country I had never visited and a very different challenge.

Before leaving the Philippines, we got in one last trip to Maya Maya for waterskiing and sun and took Cara to Tokyo for Disneyland and cherry blossoms. Then we packed up for Germany, taking Sebastian the basset hound with us.

When we left the Philippines, Coke had a 2 to 1 lead in that huge market. Instead of losing $5 million per year, the joint venture was making a $4 million profit. The Philippines had a per capita annual soft drink consumption of 134 bottles per year, compared to 39 for Thailand and 10 for Indonesia. In 1984, my last full year in the Philippines, Coke sales increased by 11 percent, despite a 5 percent drop in soft drink sales across the country and a similar drop that year in the Filipino gross domestic product. Coca-Cola was selling more concentrate to the joint bottler and the value of its stake in the venture soared. A decade after the joint venture bottler was formed, the business was worth half a billion dollars, five times its value when I arrived.

I left just as the Marcos regime began to totally unravel. Marcos was forced from power in February 1986 following the assassination of opposition leader Ninoy Aquino at the airport as he returned from exile. Marcos fled to Hawaii, where he died in 1989. Aquino's widow, Corazon, led the EDSA revolution along with Fidel Ramos. Both went on to become president. The Aquinos' son, Benigno, is the current president. Before Marcos relinquished his presidency, San Miguel was the target of a boycott by Marcos opponents because of Cojuangco's connections to the regime, causing a temporary 20 percent drop in the value of San Miguel stock.

In retrospect, the most important business lesson I can impart from my time in the Philippines is the importance—the necessity—of learning how to rally the troops. You can be the best accountant in the world, the best technician or global strategist, you can work one hundred hours a week, but if you can't motivate the men and women who are the company's frontline in the marketplace, you are not likely to succeed as a business leader. Of course, it's more complicated than that. We need superior strategies and tactics and a strong balance sheet and always, the power of the world's greatest brand, Coca-Cola. In the end, however, it's all about people.

When I look back at images of a younger version of myself in the Philippines doing pushups on the stage, wearing a general's uniform, riding in a tank, smashing Pepsi bottles against the wall amid the blaring lyrics of "Eye of the Tiger," it is a distant world from the staid Coke boardroom of later years, where I wore expensive suits and had the privilege of meeting with some of the most powerful business leaders of the world.

I now realize that without the motivational skills I developed in the tropical islands of the Philippines, I would never have been able to successfully lead Coca-Cola or any other large company.

In retrospect, I also see how important it was to have plunged into a corporate turnaround battle, which was to prove valuable when I became Chairman and CEO of the company nearly two decades later. It was risky, yes, but for any business executive, there is no greater opportunity, both in the short and long term, than transforming a money-losing operation into a profitable one.

The Philippines made my career.

Four

STAGNATION IN WEST GERMANY

There could not have been a greater contrast between the tropical Philippines with its relaxed, fun-loving atmosphere, and the often cold and rainy, sophisticated, and stoic West Germany—informality to formality, relaxed to disciplined. We moved from one extreme to another on every point of the scale.

While back in Atlanta for eight weeks of training—technically I'd been away from the Coca-Cola Company for four years—Pamela traveled to Düsseldorf, which was buried in snow. In a week she found a house for us to rent, a school for Cara, and opened bank accounts, evidence of an amazing skill set that contributed greatly to my career advancement over the years. Then Pamela flew back to the Philippines to pack up our belongings for the move to Germany. Cara was only seven and had already lived in four countries and on three continents.

I was the first non-German since 1933 to head Coca-Cola in Germany, which was vying with Japan to be the largest division in the company's international portfolio. While on a visit to the Philippines, Don Keough had offered me the new job during a meeting at the famous Manila Hotel. He wanted an outsider to shake up the business and energize a profitable but stagnant market. I was up for the challenge, even though I spoke very little German despite a one-week course I took in New York.

My new job came with the title of Division President of Central Europe, with Switzerland and Austria also part of my territory. It was a tumultuous year for Coca-Cola, which had in a bold move introduced a new, sweeter formula, New Coke, in the spring of 1985.

Consumer backlash was palpable, as I discovered while in Atlanta for my orientation on Germany. Checking in on a flight from Atlanta to Savannah for a meeting on bottler restructuring, an airline attendant saw the Coca-Cola tag on my luggage and promptly said, "I hate you. You took my Coca-Cola away. You've ruined my life."

You could feel the tension at headquarters, which was fielding similar complaints, even from bottlers who said they were ostracized at their hometown country clubs. The Coke leadership called in executives from all over the world, telling everyone in no uncertain terms to stay on message during the controversy and not to criticize New Coke.

Germany had been scheduled to be next behind the U.S. to launch New Coke but it became clear in my first meeting with the German bottlers that they wanted no part of it. I then discovered that we were about to launch Cherry Coke in Germany so I requested headquarters to delay New Coke, arguing that there wasn't anything wrong with New Coke (wink, wink), but that handling two launches at once would be too difficult. I was buying time and it worked.

New Coke had been one of the most heavily researched products of all time, and while many consumers liked the taste, the studies never detected the impact of killing the old formula, which over decades had developed an extremely strong and nostalgic following. As Keough later said, the original formula reminded many consumers of their youth, and Coke was taking that away. In fact, some believed the New Coke fiasco was a clever marketing trick since sales actually increased as lapsed users rediscovered their favorite brand. Keough has always captured the truth when he said, "We are not that dumb and we are not that smart." It was a great lesson on market research. You have to be sure you're asking the right questions in the right way in the right context. No one researched what the reaction would be if the result of New Coke was taking the old formula away. It was also a much deeper lesson: The brand belongs to the consumer. While the formula was under lock and key, what it stood for was locked into the minds of consumers. The brand was bigger than the company. Many years of history had un-equivocally defined the brand to its loyal consumers and even to its lapsed consumers.

The old formula, renamed "Classic Coke," was resurrected after about ten weeks and New Coke gradually faded away, sparing me from facing that controversy in Germany.

With that potential maelstrom averted, I began settling in to my new job and our new life. It was not easy at first, but we worked hard to connect to the local culture.

While most of the expats chose to live near the American

International School, where Cara was enrolled, Pamela and I decided to live in an all-German neighborhood. This was somewhat difficult at first since our neighbors were not prone to knocking on the door and introducing themselves. In fact, they hardly knew each other. Shortly after arriving, we held a dinner party for my direct reports and their wives; some of the wives of the senior executives had never met one another. Socializing with coworkers was not part of the culture. The dinner party was also a lesson in German punctuality. At ten minutes before the appointed arrival time, we heard the cars pull up. At two minutes to the hour, we heard the almost simultaneous opening and closing of car doors. Then the doorbell rang and there was everyone standing at our door!

At the office, managers always kept their doors closed, a part of the German psyche. I had read about German culture and its do's and don'ts. The classic American way was to make changes that alienated the culture, a big mistake. While the closed atmosphere did not match my style, the only change I made was to keep my own office door open, hoping to set an example.

With the help of Heinz Wiezorek, my German equivalent of King King, I did try to make little moves to create a more relaxed atmosphere. Senior management ate lunch each day in the executive dining room, where there was a buzzer just beneath my place at the table. In a robotic procedure symbolic of the stilted office atmosphere, I would hit the button when we were finished with the first course and the door to the kitchen would open, almost instantaneously, and a waitress would march in to clear the plates for the next course of the three-course meal. After a while, I decided to close the executive dining room, requiring executives to begin eating lunch in the canteen with everyone else. I also had the offices repainted in white and Coca-Cola's signature red, covering up the depressing dark brown color scheme. We also eliminated preferential parking spots. These may seem like minor moves but they were symbolic of a more open culture, a less hierarchal culture that I was trying to create. My view is that people judge not just by hearing what you say but by seeing what you do.

This was the era of a German terrorist group called the Red Army Faction, which killed and kidnapped leading business figures. Sadly, Alfred Herrhausen, Deutsche Bank chairman and a member of the Coca-Cola advisory board, was a victim of the Red Army Faction. I was reliably informed that my name was on the list. Our home was equipped with a panic button to the local police which we were forced to use one day after a drunk arrived at our door, shouting abuse. Police were there in ninety seconds. We were also provided with a company driver who would take Cara to and from school each day, always by varied routes. Most of the parents at the school came to believe that the driver was actually Cara's father. It took me quite a few months to learn that although the drivers may not speak English well, they understood it completely. This allowed me to build a very useful relationship with them. They would pick up visitors from Atlanta at the Frankfurt airport for the two-hour drive to Essen. As they sat in the backseat, talking about the business and about me, the drivers would listen, understanding just about every-thing that was said. It took about a year before they started relaying the stories to me and I had a wonderful accidental espio-nage operation about what executives in Atlanta were saying and thinking. Lesson: Drivers have ears.

In Germany, I faced a completely different business challenge

than I had in the Philippines. Coke overwhelmingly domi-
nated the German market and profits were good. However, sales
were stagnant, as were profits.

Part of the solution was to consolidate the 116 bottlers in
West Germany. The bottling system had been developed after
World War II, literally with bottling equipment that had been
used to ensure that U.S. soldiers had Coca-Cola on the battle-
front. During the war, Coca-Cola Germany remained intact,
managed by Max Keith. Although it was impossible during the
war to import Coca-Cola concentrate, Keith invented Fanta,
the company's first noncola product, which is now the leading
orange drink in the world, although the Italians also claim prov-
enance. In the war's aftermath, smaller bottling plants made sense
because there was a shortage of investment capital and many of
the roads and bridges were still bomb-damaged. The trip from
Essen to Düsseldorf, now a twenty-minute drive, took two hours
in the early postwar years. In those days, the cost of distribution
could actually outweigh the cost of production, so the solution
had been to build many smaller bottling plants throughout the
country. There was a bottling plant in Essen and a bottling plant
in Düsseldorf.

The German bottling system, precisely because the plants
were small and locally owned, became one of the best in the
world, trailing only Japan and the U.S. and counting among its
owners many prominent citizens, including Max Schmeling,
the former heavyweight boxing champion of the world, who
defeated Joe Louis in June 1936 and returned triumphantly to
Berlin aboard the *Hindenburg* airship, only to lose to Louis in a
rematch two years later. Max told Pamela that he had been
booked on the ill-fated final flight of the *Hindenburg* in 1937,

saved only by a last-minute change of plans. Max, who had refused to join the Nazi Party and saved the lives of two Jewish children by hiding them in his Berlin apartment, was a hero in Germany for the remainder of his long life.

Despite its lofty reputation, the German system had become a very high-cost operation by the time I arrived, lacking the economies of scale that consolidation could provide. Also, the original owners of the bottling plants were passing them on to their children, who were already wealthy; some of them drove Ferraris and Mercedes-Benzes and weren't always as focused on Coca-Cola as their parents had been. It's the classic story of family-owned businesses and one of the flaws in the franchise structure.

With a 6 to 1 lead in Germany, the strength of the Coke brand meant that we could charge a premium for our product, with our prices often 20 percent higher than Pepsi's. Yet in the long term, I knew this was unsustainable. We were facing increased competition from imports and from Pepsi. We, as a system, had to bring down our costs.

As Heinz and I went about trying to consolidate the bottlers, I found the command structure in Germany under which we worked strange and sometimes awkward. I was caught between three Germans: Klaus Putter, Claus Halle, and Eric Kreusch. Putter was head of Coke in Europe and Halle was International President. Both were based in Atlanta, but had a fractured relationship. Putter was technically my boss, but from day one Halle instructed me to report to him directly—though informally— as well as to Putter. Further complicating matters was the fact that Kreusch, my predecessor as head of Coke in Germany, had stayed on when I took over, and had been assigned to manage the bottler consolidation. This seemed to make a great deal of sense since Kreusch knew the bottling system and its owners, and the complexities of German law. Kreusch was detached from the day-to-day operations of the German business which I was undertaking with Heinz.

In German management structures, all of the top executives are referred to as *Geschäftsführer* or business leaders. Unbeknownst to me, Kreusch was portraying himself to the bottlers as the head business leader, the speaker. Although he had been demoted and was reporting to me in the Coca-Cola structure, I was told he had set himself up among the German bottlers as my superior. I was forced to go to Atlanta and explain to Halle that I believed Kreusch was undermining me. I asked for permission to let Kreusch go, and Halle approved. I then sought and received Putter's approval.

It was a tough start for my new job. I didn't speak the language, a key executive was working behind my back, and I was caught between two bosses who, although they had started in the German business within days of each other, had always had a frosty relationship.

My next task was even less pleasant: I eliminated one hundred high-cost positions in the head office, which was over-staffed and over-bureaucratized. We were not investing enough money in the marketplace, hence the stagnation. In order to free up funds, I needed to cut costs. In Germany it's very difficult to fire employees. You have to go through the Works Council and the process is laborious. A number of people who worked for me, including the head of human resources and the head of legal, told me it would be impossible. Within a year, however, it was done and the savings directed to marketing.

If there is one commonality in my career it has been the cutting of unnecessary costs to fuel marketing. (I have seen how management cuts marketing to fuel the bottom line and make their numbers, to the detriment of the business in the long term.) My approach has to a degree earned me the reputation of not being tough enough on marketing costs, and while recognizing that there is always some waste in that area, at the end of the day marketing is the most important thing we can do to fuel the brands.

In my first speech to the German bottlers, I told them, "You are looking at this Irishman who has come here from the Philippines, who knows nothing about Germany. You're looking at him and saying, 'Who is this man and why is he here?' I'll tell you why I am here. I'm here because this is a great business which is no longer performing. You are living in the past and we need to look to the future."

They thought they were the best bottlers in the world, yet there was no growth, which was indisputable. What was disputable, however, was a belief by some that we had reached the limits of growth.

"I've come to bring growth back for you and for us," I continued. "But I want to give you the good news and the bad news. The good news is that I'm a bottler and I know your business. The bad news is that I'm a bottler and I know your business."

The bottlers banged their fists on the table in a form of applause and appreciation, thawing the relationship temporarily, though many battles were yet to be fought. Germany had a very powerful Bottlers Association that was run by a bottler named Klaus Maurers. Klaus and I managed to strike up a close relationship. He was a tough negotiator but an honorable man.

Later, when I was Chairman and CEO of the company, the trust we developed during those early years would prove to be particularly valuable.

As Heinz and I began examining the bottler consolidation issue, we realized that the Coca-Cola Company had a major bargaining chip. German bottlers had been reluctant to invest in canning plants, so Coca-Cola had built most of them instead, which made Coca-Cola the owner of canning operations in Germany. Over the years, cans represented an increasing percentage of overall sales and the German bottlers regretted that they had ceded this lucrative segment of the business. Essentially, the company had two profit streams: one from concentrate as was normal, and the second from production of canned products. The bottlers only had a modest distribution margin on cans although some did own shares in some of the canning plants.

Heinz and I developed a plan: We would consolidate the 116 bottlers into one new company, which would include the lucrative canning franchises. The bottlers would receive shares in the new concern in exchange for their plants. The shares would have been much more valuable than the small bottling plants themselves, in part because of the canning franchises but also because of the enormous cost savings we calculated from consolidating the bottling operations.

Max Schmeling, the boxing champion, was well respected and he and I had developed a strong relationship, despite the fact that his English was not very good and my German was weak. On his eightieth birthday, I presented Max with a sculptured boxing glove holding a Coca-Cola bottle, made of heavyweight Krupp steel. It encapsulated Germany's solidity and Max's life as a boxer and Coke bottler.

I believe Max translated to the bottlers that I was sincere in my consolidation efforts. In the summer of 1987, Atlanta gave me approval to present the plan to the bottlers. In our initial meetings we had greater acceptance than we anticipated but it was far from universal. We felt that we had about 40 percent of the bottlers on board, another 30 percent whom we could convince, and another 30 percent who strongly opposed the plan and would never agree. Despite our optimism, the plan immediately sparked an uproar. Regardless of the obvious business logic, and the fact that it would be very lucrative for the bottlers, emotion surged.

For many of the bottlers, higher profits did not trump the loss of control over their own companies, Heinz recalled in an interview for this book. And some of the bottlers were already so wealthy, a little more money was not that tempting, particularly if it meant losing the prestige of owning a Coca-Cola bottling franchise.

"We would tell the bottler, 'Today you make five million dollars a year in profit. You could easily make seven million dollars,'" Heinz recalled. "The bottler would say, 'I don't know what I should do with the five million dollars. My family is rich. Everything is great. What will I do with the additional two million dollars?'"

Bottlers began calling Atlanta to complain, which we had expected and felt we could manage. We were wrong. Heinz and I were at a meeting in Munich when Halle called. "Stop," he told me. "You're not to go any further. You are to abandon the plan."

Heinz and I met that evening in the hotel, believing our careers were over, that we had been totally undermined by headquarters, and that we needed to resign. We both agreed to do so the next morning. Yet after sleeping on it, we decided not to. Although we had indeed been undermined, we were not going to give up so easily. We would now find another way to accomplish our goal.

Soon after, we began negotiations with the bottlers and developed a plan to lower costs while whittling the number of bottlers down to 30—not one, as originally planned. We created a central sales office, which was both more efficient and more convenient for the larger customers, who would no longer have to order from several different bottlers. And we closed some production facilities and gave the bottlers a piece of the canning business in exchange for lowering some of their product discounts. It was a compromise and like all compromises, it was a bit messy. Although the overall strategy was seen as a success in Atlanta—I *had* managed to consolidate Austria and Switzerland down to single bottlers—in Germany it got us only halfway to where we needed to be. Halfway wasn't enough, though we were able to put growth back into the business and achieve a material increase in profitability. Later, as CEO and Chairman, I finished the job that needed to be done. Today, Germany operates under a single bottler.

In another accomplishment which I viewed as significant, Heinz and I also introduced a new returnable 1.5 liter plastic bottle, which is still used in many countries. "We invented the bottle even though we did not have approval from Atlanta to do so," recalled Heinz, who succeeded me as German division manager. "We saved money in other parts of our business and paid for the development of the bottle, which was a lightweight plastic. In marketing, we touted it as the 'unbreakable bottle.'"

The bottle was extremely successful and decades ahead of its time environmentally. Retailers embraced the bottles because they contained 50 percent more content than the old one liter glass bottles. Germans were accustomed to returning bottles for deposits. They returned all empty bottles—soft drinks, mineral water, and beer—so it was already part of the culture. The new plastic bottles were washed, sanitized, and reused twenty times, greatly reducing the amount of plastic used.

Despite these achievements, there were times when I worried that my career at Coca-Cola was over.

At a gathering of supermarket executives in Nice, France, Don Keough, the company president, and Ralph Cooper, one of my peers in Europe, were there for two days. I suddenly realized that Ralph had been invited by Don to a dinner, and I was ignored. I thought Don was snubbing me because of the bottler restructuring and mentioned it to his executive assistant, John White, who managed to get me into one final lunch. Still, I believed I was getting the cold shoulder from North Avenue.

At the airport in Nice, I ran into Michael J. O'Connor, a giant in the supermarket industry and close friend of Keough, who had founded the Retail Research Council in the U.S. I became good friends with Michael while serving on the Research Council in Europe and he was someone I trusted and confided in.

"I just got stiffed by Don," I told Michael. "I think it's over."

At this point in my career, other companies were approaching me to discuss job offers and some of the positions were quite attractive, such as president of the Guinness beer empire, based in London. I told Michael I might start looking around.

Michael assured me that I had it all wrong and that my career was on track. "You are part of the future of this company," he said. "Stay around."

He was right and there is a business lesson there: Hypersensitivity can be hazardous to your career. As you advance up the ladder in a corporation, it is possible to see phantoms everywhere that in your perception are out to destroy your career; almost always it's your imagination trying to get the better of you.

While I perceived Don Keough as snubbing me, it was, in fact, a simple oversight. A year later, he asked me to lead a task force evaluating Coke's operation in Brazil, then managed by Jorge Giganti. North Avenue complained that Giganti was not communicating well with headquarters, that he had a crazy idea about sponsoring the bankrupt Brazilian soccer league. Behind it all, however, was the basic fact that growth was stagnant. After arriving in Rio, I asked Jorge for his side of the story. "It's fine," he said, later adding, "I only phone Atlanta once a month."

Within the first hour, I had discovered the core of the problem: lack of communication. We spent the week there and validated that the soccer sponsorship was actually a good idea. For only $1 million, all the soccer teams in Brazil would be wearing the Coca-Cola logo. This was Brazil and this was soccer. We would have been crazy to have turned down that sponsorship. A lack of trust and a lack of communication between Giganti and headquarters had placed a cloud over the deal. I disagreed with only one of Giganti's decisions, which was to allow the Coke bottlers to also sell beer. A visit to one bottling plant convinced me of this. The beer trucks outside the plant were shiny and new while the Coca-Cola trucks were a disgrace, the paint faded and chipped. Giganti and more important, some of the bottlers, had fallen in love with a new skirt—beer—and were ignoring the more profitable mainstay, Coca-Cola.

I returned to Atlanta and presented my findings to the company senior management team led by Keough and Claus Halle. "I actually think this is very simple," I told the group. "You're half the problem and Jorge is half the problem. You're talking past each other. At the end of the day, it's as simple as that." I then, point by point, went through the other outstanding issues, largely agreeing with the Brazilian strategies.

I told them further that Jorge had agreed to begin calling Atlanta once a week and to be absolutely transparent about what he was doing. "I think it's going to work," I added. It did. Communication and trust often drive decision-making as much as logic.

For the first year in Germany, my family and I were miserable, but that would change totally as we learned to appreciate the warmth of the people. There is nothing superfluous in German friendship. German friends are real friends. We ended up making some really great friends and keep in touch with them even to this day. In Germany, there is a tradition that when you become close, a family will literally "propose," asking you to become "du" friends. Du is the German word for "you" reserved for family and close friends as opposed to the more formal "sie." When you are asked to become a "du" friend, both couples link arms and drink a toast of German Sekt (champagne). It's quite a big deal. We made three "du" friends in Germany while we were there, all outside the Coca-Cola community.

On one occasion, we went with one of our du friends to a particularly memorable dinner at the Bavarian castle of the Count of Thurn und Taxis, who was a member of a royal family that had made a fortune developing the German postal service.

The count needed a successor and was married to a young woman named Gloria von Thurn und Taxis, who was totally outrageous and featured in every German magazine. At the time she was in her late twenties and her hair was dyed pink. The count was forty years her senior.

It was a very formal dinner with ornate candelabras on the table and footmen wearing their royal livery. After dinner, we retired to the basement and the castle bowling alley which was old, wooden, and warped. On the wall were the names of the bowlers who had scored strikes, dating back to the 1800s, with royal names in gold, commoners in black. The count was sitting in a corner, rather inebriated, with spiffy young men fawning over him. His young wife, a singer in a pop band, decided to give a live performance with a song to her husband that was basically a sexual taunt. The cellar was filled with serious business executives along with young and trendy German society on the dance floor. We managed to slide out early at 3:30 A.M. with a glimpse of a side of German life that fascinated us but to which we did not belong.

We loved the order and discipline of Germany, although we hated the fact that shops closed at noon on Saturdays. For example, there was a pond near our house and we'd go there regularly to buy fresh trout, though never on Sundays when almost everything was closed. Our house in France was a twelve-hour drive away so we were able to spend more time there as well as in many wonderful European cities. Pamela wanted a Mercedes 280 SLC and we bought one, even though some people told us a certain "lady of the evening" drove the same model. However, we decided that since it was the car Pamela wanted she should have it. And I could use the extra tax-free income!

We spent some weekends along the Rhine River with its absolute picture-book scenery, once staying in a twelfth-century renovated castle with an owner who also looked like he had come out of the twelfth century. There was another memorable weekend on Sylt, the fashionable North Sea island that almost anyone who is anyone has visited. The people are easy to identify and remember; as you wander the beaches, you can't help but notice a complete absence of any swimwear, although there were *some* people who were fully clothed, including ourselves. Pamela noted, correctly, that most of the people who had their clothes off were a little too old to be interesting. I remember standing, suitably clad, in a line to get ice cream between two rather naked, very brown, slightly protruding ladies. Two elderly couples, both stark naked, approached each other on the beach. Apparently friends, they kissed each other on the cheek and greeted one another in the third person while their extremities flapped with their movements. Despite baring all, they were not yet "du" friends.

We were even able to make a day trip behind the Berlin Wall on a cold winter day in 1987. Pamela, Cara, and I joined a German colleague at Coke, Georg Fleischer, and his wife and daughter. Georg, who escaped from East Germany after World War II by jumping over a barbwire fence, was in charge of the communist countries in Eastern Europe as well as Turkey, a very small division that dealt primarily in countertrade since communist currency was not convertible on the world market. Under this arrangement, Coca-Cola would trade for a product made by the communist country and would then sell that product in the West, creating a credit which allowed the import of the concentrate to produce our brands. It was a very difficult and awkward process since there were so few Eastern bloc products that could be sold easily in the West. (One notable exception was the Russian vodka, Stolichnaya, landed exclusively, and unfortunately, by Pepsi.)

We hired drivers to take us across the border in separate cars, Georg and his family taking one checkpoint since they were German citizens. My family and I went through the infamous Checkpoint Charlie, a chilling experience with an extensive, tense search that lasted nearly forty-five minutes. All your money had to be converted into East German marks, and if the money was unspent you were not allowed to bring it out of East Germany on your return to the West.

Georg took us on a tour of the neighborhood where he lived as a child. There were still bombed-out areas, more than forty years after the war. Georg had two sisters still living in East Berlin who were married to senior officials in the communist party.

"Theoretically, we could walk around the corner here and see your sister and brother-in-law," I said to Georg. "What would you do if that happened?"

"We would walk past each other," he replied. "It's not in my interest or Coca-Cola's interest to have any interaction with them whatsoever. And it's certainly not in their interest." It was the most chilling feeling, the very idea of walking past one's own sister. After the Wall fell, I asked Georg if he had linked up with his family. "Yes," he said. "But I do not see them anymore and we have nothing in common. We are different people."

We toured East Berlin, eating lunch at a leading hotel that

was nevertheless very low-quality and sparse. We wanted to spend our East German marks before we returned but there was very little to buy. We finally found some rubbishy souvenirs to purchase. And then it hit me: There was no economy in East Germany. There was no advertising. It was gray and dark with no ambience. How was that sustainable? We went back through the border and I felt a tremendous relief at getting out. You really did feel oppressed behind the Berlin Wall.

At age nine, Cara suddenly decided that she wanted to be an English girl in an English boarding school, and enrolled in Moira House School in Eastbourne. We missed her dreadfully and visited on weekends, but in early 1989 it was time to move to yet another continent, and this time Cara traded her British accent for a Southern drawl.

While I had viewed my efforts in Germany as a partial failure since we had never totally consolidated the bottlers, Atlanta apparently felt otherwise. In the fall of 1988, just three months after I had helped resolve the friction between headquarters and Brazil, I was offered a position in Atlanta as a group president for all of Eastern and Northern Europe, the Soviet Union, Africa, and the Middle East, seventy-nine countries in all.

We were sorry to leave Germany. It had grown on us during our time there. Yet for the first time since South Africa we would have a permanent home. Pamela and I had always liked Atlanta when we'd visited and rated it as one of America's nicest cities, with its wonderful warm climate most of the year, abundance of trees and lakes, and Southern hospitality.

Right before leaving Germany, Georg, who would now report to me, took me on a tour of Turkey, one of the countries in my new territory, to see where real opportunities lay and to meet someone he had a high regard for. The man was a young, up-and-coming region manager named Muhtar Kent. I had no way of knowing it at the time, but Muhtar would soon become one of my most valuable lieutenants.

The world was about to change very quickly.

Five

THE WALL FALLS

S hortly after moving to Atlanta, I found myself on a company plane to Saudi Arabia, summoned to a meeting with Prince Faisal.

Saudi Arabia ejected Coca-Cola in 1968 during the Arab League boycott of companies doing business with Israel. Although the boycott was slowly fading and Coca-Cola was sponsoring the World Youth Soccer Tournament in Saudi Arabia in February 1989, a legal dispute blocked us from building a bottling plant there. We even had to obtain an import license to ship product in for the tournament.

The Kaki family, which owned the Saudi bottling franchise before the boycott, claimed it still had the rights, which Coca-Cola disputed. The legal case was complicated by the fact that in Coke's absence, Kaki produced its own brand called Kaki Cola, and Coca-Cola, had unfortunately, supplied a cola concentrate, although not the original formula, for the drink.

With the boycott ending, Coca-Cola awarded the bottling

franchise to the very reputable and wealthy Olayan family but the legal suit with the Kaki family was progressing very slowly. Geoff Unsworth, who was in charge of Coke's Middle Eastern operations at the time, did not endear himself to me when he repeated former White House Press Secretary Marlin Fitzwater's quote, "When you're dealing with the Middle East, two thousand years is the normal wait for something to happen." Sorry, but that was a bit too long of a wait for me.

We met Prince Faisal in his office, a huge opulent room. His desk was on a raised platform so we were literally looking up at him. He proceeded to deliver a lecture: It was fine for Coca-Cola to come in for the soccer tournament (which Prince Faisal was personally directing) though we would never be allowed to permanently reenter Saudi unless we partnered with the prince's preferred partners, not the Olayans. The prince wanted the business and was absolutely hostile, at times dropping veiled threats into our conversation.

We reported back to the Olayans and were assured by the company patriarch, Suliman Olayan, that we should not be concerned. "He's been given the World Youth Tournament to run because he's not really one of the influential princes," Suliman said. "This, too, will pass."

The prince contacted us once again a few months later but we were unable to schedule a meeting and never heard from him again. Suliman was right, it went away. Meanwhile, the Kaki suit made its way torturously through the Saudi courts, and at one point we had to appear before the Saudi Minister of Justice. For two hours we sat with a senior member of the Olayan family while the minister heard all the other cases. Some of them were rather tragic. There was an eighteen-year-old girl married to a really wizened old man, a forced marriage. She claimed that he had beaten her, yet the minister brusquely sent her home with no relief. It was like a medieval court.

When we were called, the minister asked us a few questions and eventually ruled in our favor. The Olayan family has the bottling franchise to this day, overseen by Suliman's youngest daughter, Lubna. While in Saudi Arabia, we visited a private home where the Johnnie Walker Black Label flowed—along with the best wine—and everyone stood around the swimming pool drinking. The duplicity of the society was absolutely apparent. Not surprisingly, there were two sets of rules in this conservative, Muslim country. That was my first introduction to Saudi Arabia, which was not initially a positive one, and Saudi indeed turned out to be a tough market for Coke. Pepsi had entered the Israeli market in 1992 only after the Arab boycott was over. So while Coke was in exile, Pepsi had become deeply entrenched in Middle Eastern markets like Saudi Arabia.

After the boycott ended, we hoped to initially gain a 20 percent market share in Saudi but fell short with only 9 percent, underutilizing our large new bottling plant. It was a miscalculation on my part. We were losing money but believed that if we could attack Pepsi's profit center in Saudi Arabia, it would limit Pepsi's investments in other countries in the region such as Jordan, Bahrain, and Dubai, where Coke was also struggling to rebuild. The Middle East was to provide me with many headaches over the next few years, and even today, Coke still trails Pepsi in some of the region's countries. Egypt, where we negotiated the privatization of the bottler, was one where we achieved our vision, but I underestimated the strength of the Pepsi system in countries such as Saudi Arabia.

Egypt had ejected Coca-Cola in 1967 during the Arab boycott but relented in 1979 following the Camp David Accords. The government still controlled the soft drink industry, with Pepsi leading in Cairo and Coke ahead outside the capital. Egypt later privatized the industry and I traveled to Cairo to gauge the challenge and inspect the assets the company would be purchasing from the government in a joint venture with the Alhak family. This was Egypt's first privatization since the nationalization era of Nasser. The Coke bottling plant in Cairo was in terrible shape, more run down than those in the Philippines when I first arrived there. Worse, I spotted a building adjoining the plant that was adorned with a Coca-Cola sign. "It's just another building we own," an Egyptian government official told me. Yet something in the tone of his reply made me suspicious. After further research, I discovered the building was a brothel. Although it was probably far more profitable than the bottling plant, we told Egyptian officials, "The Coca-Cola Company isn't buying a brothel." We bought the bottling plant but not the brothel property.

I focused on building sales in both the Middle East and Africa. I believed Coca-Cola had ignored Africa in particular and that there was huge growth potential there. That proved to be correct, although it has taken an enormous amount of work to achieve.

Early 1989 produced signs that apartheid in South Africa might be thawing. President F. W. de Klerk was clearly softening his position, though it was still a whites-only government and Nelson Mandela remained imprisoned. Coca-Cola had divested in 1986, moved the concentrate plant to nearby Swaziland, and signed a licensing agreement with a newly formed, entirely independent South African company, National Beverage

Services. The contract gave Coke a repurchase option when and if apartheid fell.

National Beverages was managed by a former Coca-Cola executive, Sandy Allan, an energetic and knowledgeable (but stubborn) man who I felt did not always dot all the i's or cross all the t's, which would become an issue later in his career in implementing an antitrust settlement with the European Commission. Shortly before I left Germany for Atlanta, I phoned Sandy to tell him that in my new position as group president, I would oversee the relationship with National Beverages. "No, you won't," he replied. "Nobody does."

His boasts of independence slowly softened as the political climate in South Africa evolved and he could foresee Coca-Cola returning to exercise the repurchase option. In March of 1989, I asked Sandy to come to Atlanta and conduct a review of National Beverages. I knew all the South African bottlers, and they were telling me that Sandy was too autocratic and they wanted Coke to return with new management. At the same time, Carl Ware, a Coca-Cola public affairs executive and former president of the Atlanta City Council, was working with Bishop Desmond Tutu and other members of the opposition through a South African foundation Coca-Cola had established. Through these channels, Carl, an African American, gained invaluable information on the political winds in South Africa and built valuable and powerful relationships that would serve the company well. This was a source of friction with Sandy Allan, but the company was on a dual track in preparing for a new South Africa. Without Carl and his work, the standing of the company could have been greatly diminished. I maintained a close relationship with Carl and once visited the South Georgia farm where his family had worked as sharecroppers and which he now proudly owns. Carl walked five miles to school each way and was passed daily by the bus carrying the white students. While he was often abused by these students, Carl fondly remembered his father's relationship with local white farmers.

On one trip to Africa, I returned to Zambia for a very emotional visit. Pamela was with me and had been reluctant to go back, not wanting to see how Zambia had deteriorated in the sixteen years since our departure. Zambia was indeed run down and depressing, a very pleasant land with an economy ruined by extreme mismanagement. Yet it was heartwarming to greet my old colleagues, some of whom broke into tears. I was shocked, however, to learn that so many friends had died. This was Africa before the HIV/AIDS epidemic had fully swept the continent, yet life expectancy was still very low. We shouldn't have been surprised that so many of our old friends were no longer there, but it was still very, very sad.

At a bottler's conference in Nairobi, I spoke from my heart, not as a Coca-Cola executive visiting from Atlanta, but as someone who lived twenty-six years of his life in Africa.

Mike Hall, who had been my marketing manager in Australia and was now in charge of Africa, delivered a very powerful speech before mine, which I thought would be a tough act to follow. So instead of standing behind the podium, I sat on the edge of the stage, my legs dangling.

"I'm home," I told the bottlers. "Home is Zambia, but home is Africa. There is a magic about Africa that will never leave me. It is encapsulated by that magical aroma that is released from the arid earth that has not seen rain in four months. This is rebirth. The rain has fallen. We are going to regrow this business just like the maize grows when the rain falls."

The bottlers unexpectedly broke into applause. It was a very powerful moment. For both Pamela and I, the years we lived in Africa, those formative years, haven't made us Africans, of course, but in many ways we feel like children of Africa. Hardly a year goes by without us taking some vacation time on the continent.

After the bottler conference, Mike Hall and I, along with John Belcher, another Coca-Cola executive in Africa, traveled to Ethiopia, which was then just emerging from a long and brutal war over independence for Eritrea. Coca-Cola had a bottling plant in Asmara on the coast that had been knocked out of commission during the war, and we were scheduled to meet with Isaias Afwerki, the Eritrean freedom fighter, to see if we could get it up and running again. Afwerki was going to be the new president of Eritrea, and Asmara would be the capital of the new nation.

We flew into Addis Ababa, the capital of Ethiopia. Since the war had only recently ended, the U.S. ambassador had not yet returned to the country. Our plane was among the first aircraft in there since the revolution.

We drove from the airport to the Hilton hotel, passing burnt-out tanks and cars and young men walking around with AK-47s. We had a guard in our car with an AK-47 protecting us. At the Hilton, John had arranged for us to meet with a contact, the classic Mr. Fixit in Africa. The honorary U.S. consul general, an Ethiopian, joined us. He was amazed that we were able to make it into the country as the United States had not decided to bring in its ambassador yet. This was still very dangerous territory.

Finally, we got in an old Mercedes-Benz, which had one shock absorber that was clearly not working. There were three of us in the back, Mike Hall, John Belcher, and I. Mr. Fixit squeezed in the front with the driver and the guy with the AK-47.

We arrived at a house surrounded by a six-foot-tall concrete wall and four feet of barbed wire on top with big steel gates. There were guards outside. We were ushered into the house and were seated in a very large, dimly lit room to wait for Afwerki. Twenty minutes passed. I was getting quite nervous. My palms were sweaty. I'm now thinking I really made a mistake. Finally, Afwerki arrives. We shake hands. I had the foresight to dry my hands. Yet he had a very sweaty palm. I suddenly realized that he was more nervous than I was. He told me he had never met a foreign businessman.

I started to feel as if I was in charge of the meeting and I could see Afwerki visibly relaxing as I talked about my view of Africa and how the continent had a great future. John Belcher then detailed what we needed to get the plant running in Asmara, including spare parts and a landing strip for the corporate aircraft. We reached agreement, shook hands, and happily got out of that walled compound. Eight weeks later, we were manufacturing Coca-Cola in Asmara.

For Coca-Cola, which operates in 200 countries, these types of meetings come with the territory. There are constant wars and revolutions, natural and man-made disasters. More often than not, Coca-Cola is the last company to leave, if it leaves at all, and the first to return, a record of which the company and its executives are quite proud. Yet it is not always easy to do this and is often accompanied by many anxious moments.

I discovered that Nigeria was a particularly troubled market, with absolutely abysmal conditions at the bottling plants. A good quality score is in the 90s but the plant in Lagos scored a 6, an absolute disgrace. Andrew David, a Greek Cypriot whose family owned a majority interest in the Nigerian bottling franchise, disputed those findings, saying his own inspectors had calculated a quality score in the 80s. "Are you calling my people liars?" Andrew said to me when I challenged his assertion and warned him that I had the authority to shut down the plant. We agreed to inspect the plant together with a group of technicians and as we were driving there, we passed two dead bodies along the road, apparently a common sight since none of the drivers bothered to stop. The inspection proved Andrew's numbers wrong and the next morning at breakfast he was stone-faced and refused to talk to me as we toured another plant. I insisted that we have breakfast together the next day and there was a breakthrough. We developed a plan for revamping the business, bringing in new management both at the bottler and on Coke's side. Andrew and I became very close friends after that confrontation and I later worked for him in Europe as part of a bottler merger we undertook. I was one of those whom he nominated to deliver a eulogy at his funeral in Athens. It was a sad affair as he was a great friend and great Coke bottler.

The lesson I will never forget from that confrontation with Andrew is that a business leader should never be frightened by conflict, and should always find a good, honest solution that is pragmatic, not bullheaded. There were times in my career when I took the bullheaded approach and it was always a mistake.

Back home in Atlanta, our family adjusted quickly, and really liked the American South. Cara thrived in her new school,
Pace Academy. Yet we noticed that there was less interaction
with Coca-Cola employees outside the office than there had
been in the many outposts where we had been earlier stationed.
This was home base and Coke employees were anchored in
their schools, churches, and neighborhoods and therefore less
reliant on each other. Also, I had reached a very high rank in
the company and there was a palpable difference in how lower-
level employees reacted to me. I remembered that Christmas
Eve in Johannesburg when I was having drinks and discussing
politics with my coworkers at the Sunnyside Park Hotel. That
type of camaraderie is often missing when you are a group
president. There is truth to the adage, "It's lonely at the top."

With a territory that stretched from Iceland to South Africa
and across to the far eastern USSR, half my time was spent away
from Atlanta. The travel was brutal and the time away from
home difficult for Pamela and Cara. "I miss you," Pamela wrote
in a message to me that she placed in my diary on July 11, 1989.
Yet we tried whenever possible to offset the travel and hard work
with family time and fun. I promised Cara that I would be with
her on her thirteenth birthday, but I had a mandatory meeting
in London that day. So I arranged for Cara to fly to London for
the weekend. When Cara turned sixteen she and I took a trip
to Uganda to see gorillas in the wild.

I made my first trip to Moscow to set up a representative office there for Coca-Cola, considered such a major accomplishment that we held a celebratory dinner. My accommodations
reminded me somewhat of the Crested Crane Hotel in Zambia,
the inn where I had been forced to share a bed with a coworker

so many years earlier, and where we had been served the same piece of tough meat at dinner and the next morning at breakfast. The Moscow hotel was not much better. The towels were good if you had an itchy back but in terms of absorption of water, very inefficient. The curtains in the room hardly blocked the light.

Under the countertrade arrangement at the time, Coke would ship a small amount of concentrate to the state-owned bottling plants and would receive Soviet-made Lada cars that we would sell in Great Britain for hard currency. The cars were so poorly constructed, it would require three days of modifications in Great Britain before they could be sold. Pepsi, of course, had the much better countertrade product: Stolichnaya vodka. We were losing money in the Soviet Union, but maintaining a foothold for the future. This, to a slightly lesser degree, was the situation throughout the entire communist bloc in Europe.

Then, the future arrived, on November 9, 1989. The Berlin Wall fell.

I watched the event on CNN like most everyone else. Heinz Wiezorek, who had succeeded me as region manager in Germany, was traveling in the U.S. when the Wall fell, but the company reacted quickly to the historic moment, with two bottlers in West Berlin opening their warehouses and giving free cases of Coca-Cola to East Germans who poured across the border in Trabis, tiny cars literally made of plastic.

"There were thousands of cars per day just circling the warehouse, which showed very clearly the hunger they had for Coca-Cola," Heinz recalled.

The question instantly arose: Would the bottlers in West Germany service this vast new East German territory or would the company create a new bottler in the East? Old issues about bottler consolidation resurfaced.

I arrived in Berlin in January 1990, retrieving a piece of the Wall for Cara as a souvenir. The change in atmosphere was unbelievable. Doug Ivester, who was then head of Coke in Europe, and I met with senior East German officials, all of whom had submitted their resignations and were working on the transition. On my 1987 visit behind the Wall, one could see that the citizens were deeply afraid of the communist government. Now it was the communist officials who were in fear. They were literally sweating during our meeting, their roles in the new order now completely uncertain.

"The West German bottlers would have loved if I had sold them the East," said Heinz. "However, there was no West German bottler who wanted to buy the total." The result would have been further fracturing of the system, the opposite of the goal both Heinz and I had been striving for, which was a single German bottler.

As the West German bottlers began selling in East Germany, sometimes out of makeshift tents in empty parking lots, Heinz flew to Atlanta and asked for $450 million to build a company-owned bottler in the East. I fully agreed with Heinz. While Ivester was a strong proponent, there was some initial opposition at North Avenue. "There was a time when (company president) Don Keough said to me, 'Sell it to the West German bottlers, don't invest,' " Heinz recalled.

This was typical of Don's management style. He would always ask tough questions before supporting a major investment, hoping to reveal any doubts or flaws in the plan. He was a bear at first, but once the decision was made, he would support you, even if the results later proved to be unfavorable. It was a great lesson and one I always tried to follow.

The East German venture, which I handed over to the Europe Group, indeed seemed like a risky one particularly since there was no way at that point to convert the East German mark, and no way to predict what the exchange rate would be once the currency was convertible. This was a risk we would have to take in all of the former Eastern bloc countries.

Resistance diminished after Don and other top Coke executives toured East Germany and saw the progress the company had achieved in only a few weeks: Vending machines and fountain dispensers had already started to permeate the country. On the day Coca-Cola announced the East German investment, Coke stock jumped several points. Wall Street's optimism was justified when the currency was finally converted.

"We had a huge amount of money sitting in the bank," recalled Heinz. "I will never forget one time when Claus Halle came and said, 'Do you know you have seventy-three million East German marks sitting in your bank account?'"

Less than three weeks after the Wall fell, I was in Moscow to celebrate a new symbol of the rapidly changing times. In sub-zero temperatures, my legs shaking from the cold, I turned a switch that illuminated a twenty-by-forty-foot red neon Coca-Cola sign in Pushkin Square. It was the first neon sign in the Soviet Union. Up to that point there had been no need for advertising because all businesses were state-owned. The future looked brighter indeed.

On January 31, 1990, I attended the opening of the first

McDonald's in the Soviet Union, across Pushkin Square from the new Coca-Cola sign. The opening illustrated more than any event before it the absolute hunger and thirst citizens of the Eastern bloc had for the West. Thousands of customers waited outside in the cold for hours to get in. In that first day, the restaurant served thirty thousand people, a record for McDonald's, and the rush did not abate. Even years later, there would be as many as five thousand people in line, regardless of the weather.

This was a huge breakthrough not only for McDonald's and Coca-Cola, but for all Western business, engineered beautifully by a McDonald's executive from Canada, George Cohon, after a chance meeting with Soviet officials during the 1976 Olympics in Montreal.

For the first time, foreigners were allowed to stay at the President Hotel, thanks to Cohon's breakthrough. It was an average hotel by Western standards but a big step above the poorly maintained hotel where I had stayed on my previous visit. Every floor had a woman who would hand you a room key and record the time you left and returned. There was a room at the end of the hallway and occasionally the door would be open and you could see a man wearing headphones, clearly monitoring the listening devices planted in each room. When you had a really important conversation to make, you literally took a walk in the park.

McDonald's scheduled a tour of its new factory that supplied the new restaurant and Willie Van Eupen, Coke's region manager in the Soviet Union, rented a stretch limo to transport the Coca-Cola executives, including company President Don Keough, a clearly lavish gesture that would have embarrassed all of us before one of our largest clients, McDonald's. There was no time to get another car, so we halted the limo two blocks away and trudged through the snow to the factory, hiding away the limo.

That night there was a huge celebratory dinner at the Kremlin, complete with a fashion show and music from the band of the Kremlin Guard. I was sitting at a table with Don Keough and other top executives when Craig Cohon, George's son who worked for Coca-Cola's fountain division in Atlanta, approached me. He had hooked up with one of the Russian models, telling her he was an American movie mogul, and asked me if I would go along with the ruse. I agreed and as we were talking to a group of models, the Kremlin band broke into a rendition of "A Hard Day's Night" by the Beatles. You're in the Kremlin. There's Beatles music. You have to dance to it. Craig grabbed one model, I grabbed the other, and we danced. We were having fun, dancing, and suddenly I looked up and there's another woman, a beautiful blond, waving at me. It was my wife. I sheepishly waved back.

After the dinner, Pamela and I joined a group back at the hotel bar, including the models and Moscow City Council members, Don Keough and others. Pamela gave up around 1 A.M. I kicked on to around 2:30. I have a photograph somewhere of Don and myself, Craig Cohon and his brother and the Russian models. All of us looked rather the worse for wear. The larger point is that relations with the Soviet Union were improving. Here we were having fun in a hotel reserved for the Soviet hierarchy, which our tour guides had never been inside. The opening of the first McDonald's, along with the Coca-Cola neon sign on Pushkin Square, was a harbinger of better days ahead.

I had to learn quickly how to endure an old business ritual in the Soviet Union: the ubiquitous vodka toast, which requires you to balance the vodka glass on the edge of one hand, raise the glass to your lips, and lower it without dropping it. First, they would make a toast and you would knock back a shot of vodka. Then you would be expected to make a toast and it would go on for a dozen rounds or more. The idea, it seemed, was to get you drunk enough so that you would do something stupid. This could be at any time of the day or night. The day after the opening of McDonald's, Don Keough and I had a meeting at the Kremlin with the minister of foreign economic affairs. It was 7:30 A.M. "We have to have a toast," the minister said, bringing out brandy from his desk drawer for a round of toasts before breakfast.

I developed a survival system. Everyone during the toasts had water as a chaser. I would ask for a Coke as well. I would knock back the first two shots of vodka in the normal fashion. From then on, I would spit most of the vodka back into the water glass, chasing the toast with my Coke to make it appear normal. I was able to essentially drink less than half the volume of the others. I remember one Russian complimenting me, "You can really drink your vodka. You're strong!"

The Soviet Union was slow to adapt to capitalism, but progress was rapid in the smaller countries of Eastern Europe. One absolute gem was Romania, which was virgin territory for both Coca-Cola and Pepsi. Just two months after the February 1990 overthrow of Romania's communist president, Nicolae Ceaușescu, a letter arrived on Roberto Goizueta's desk from Ion Staminichi, who ran two state-owned bottling plants in

Romania and wanted the Coca-Cola franchise. The letter was passed to me and from me to Muhtar Kent, who was deputy division president in Essen, Germany. We set up a meeting with Staminichi and were impressed. Staminichi had never buckled to Ceauşescu and yet had managed to survive. Although the plants he ran were old and really run down, and produced only flavored drinks and not cola, this was an opportunity to be first in the door. Georg Fleischer and I made a pitch to Don Keough for $8.5 million for a joint venture, arguing that it was a meager investment to be first on the ground in a European country of 20 million people. Don pounded the table, as he was sometimes known to do.

"You're asking me to invest $8.5 million of Coca-Cola's money in Romania and you don't even know how to get that money out of Romania?" he said.

"Yes, Don," I replied. "I believe things will change. For $8.5 million, to be first in against Pepsi, to capture that market, is the right thing to do. It's leadership and we need to be the leader."

Don looked at me and said, "OK, go do it." The message was: Don't wilt. Don, a brilliant manager, was trying to ensure I was committed. In the end, that was more important than Don's own opinion of the deal, since I would be the one making sure it worked. "OK, Don, we'll deliver," I said. Romania has proven to be a very profitable market for Coke, with strong leadership over Pepsi.

As we invested quickly in one Eastern European country after the other, Muhtar was my most valuable lieutenant on the ground. "We took some risks and made some things work fast for the company in Eastern Europe," Muhtar recalled. "We made sure that people up the chain knew what we were doing so that there was never a surprise. We pulled the bureaucracy with us, so to speak. They were hanging on to the train."

Coke decided to invest in Romania before the country had even written a foreign investment law, Muhtar recalled.

"We were buying a factory and we were going to put a two-year supply of concentrate in as our equity," said Muhtar. "Don asked, 'What are you going to do after two years?' We had faith. We knew it would take care of itself. It was a very genuine belief that all of those countries, as the Berlin Wall fell, were actually going to fall into a capitalist system, sooner or later, one way or the other, and they all needed foreign investment, they all needed free-floating currency. It was a risk worth taking."

Every country had its own story, its own leaders, its own way of doing business.

"In Poland, there was no private ownership of land," said Muhtar. "How are we going to get land for the first Coca-Cola plant in Eastern Europe? We did a deal with the Catholic Church because the church was the largest land owner in Poland and had been for centuries. Even the Soviets, no matter how much they pressured the Polish government, could not get the Polish government to confiscate land from the church because it would have been considered heresy."

We signed a deal with the church to lease land for the first bottling plant. "That land to this day is still leased from the church," said Muhtar.

We built the new bottling plant in Gdynia, a few miles from Poland's shipbuilding center, Gdansk, where the Solidarity Movement had been born. Don Keough flew in for the opening along with other executives from Atlanta. It was Coke's first new bottling plant in Eastern Europe, a very big deal. That Sunday morning, Don informed us that we were all going to mass at the historic St. Brigid's Church, which counted among its parishioners Solidarity leader Lech Walesa. The pastor at St. Brigid's was Henryk Jankowski, Solidarity's chaplain.

They seated the Coke delegation in the first row of the packed church. We couldn't understand Jankowski's entire sermon, but it was laced with the term "Coca-Cola." It sounded almost as if he was telling members of the congregation that if they didn't drink at least one Coke every morning, they would be sentenced to eternal damnation. We learned later that he was detailing the economic benefits of the new plant in bringing jobs to the community. It was an education on the benefits of capitalism, straight from the Catholic Church.

Soon, it was time to collect the church offering. Don, an American Catholic, placed U.S. dollars in the plate and smiling, passed it to me, an Irish Protestant. I put my money in and handed it to Georg Fleischer, a German Lutheran. Next was Andrew David, the Greek Orthodox bottler who was scouting investments in Eastern Europe. He passed it on to Muhtar, an American-born Turk and Muslim. The last member of our delegation was Danny Moskovitz, an American Jew. Here was the Coca-Cola delegation and it was totally ecumenical, long before the burst of globalization of recent years. This is why the Coca-Cola Company is so fascinating. It's a United Nations, a functioning and profitable United Nations.

The transformation of Eastern Europe continued, country by country, with Muhtar leading the charge through unstructured and uncharted territory.

"Travel was often very difficult," Muhtar recalled. "I shared a hotel room with a Chinese guy in Albania. I turned the light on and there was a guy in the other bed. I thought I had the wrong room and went down to the lobby, but they said, 'No, that's your room.'"

We were corporate cowboys, and reporters sometimes described me as the Indiana Jones of Coca-Cola. "We were pioneers in an environment that was just beginning to become less hostile to capitalism and free enterprise," said Muhtar. "The same thing has happened in China over the last ten years. I believe in the second decade of this century, a similar boom and opening will happen in Africa, which has a billion young people."

Amid the opening of Eastern Europe, Muhtar and I faced an ugly stand-down with a bottler in Turkey. It's rare for Coca-Cola to revoke a bottler's franchise. Only in extreme circumstances is this done. Normally, the company tries to work with the bottler to resolve the problems. The Turkish bottler, the Has Group, controlled 80 percent of the volume in that country, and after the owner, a renowned and successful businessman, died, the quality of the operations began to deteriorate. The owner's widow put her partner in charge and he was hostile as we tried to help him improve. In a meeting in Istanbul with Muhtar and me, sitting on the partner's desk was a pistol, which I felt was a clear attempt at intimidation.

We summoned the bottler's owners to Atlanta for a meeting and I instructed security to bring the boyfriend into the building through the basement and give him a thorough pat down; not the usual greeting for a major bottler, but in this case it was necessary to show the partner that we didn't trust him.

During this same time period, Muhtar's BMW was destroyed in an Istanbul car bombing. Fortunately, he was not injured and no link with the Turkish bottler was ever established. Yet these were tense days indeed, even more so when the bottler's widow began lobbying the wife of Turkey's president, Turgut Özal, to intervene on her behalf. Muhtar arranged for us to meet with the president and we arrived at his office on January 17, 1991, just as the U.S. began bombing Iraq, the launch of the first Gulf War. Özal was watching the war unfold on CNN.

He gave us a whiskey and the three of us watched it. "He was getting calls from President Bush," Muhtar recalled. "In front of us, he talked to Bush twice because the line got cut the first time. In between, we were trying to tell him that we meant good for Turkey, we were here to invest. We were not trying to be harmful to anyone."

When I asked President Özal why he was watching CNN when at the same time he was talking to President Bush, he laughed and said that Bush was also watching CNN as the network delivered information quicker than the White House bureaucracy.

Coke revoked the Turkish franchise, parted amicably with the Has Group, and built our own bottling plants. Today, Turkey is one of the company's strongest growth markets.

The only other bottler dispute of that magnitude during my career developed in Norway and Sweden in the mid 1990s. I learned in a newspaper story that Orkla, the bottler in part of Norway, had taken over the Pripps Brewery, which was the Coke bottler in Sweden. Coca-Cola had never approved the sale, a clear contractual breach. Furthermore, Orkla wanted only the Coke franchise in Sweden, not Fanta and Sprite, which they would replace with their own brands. We refused, prompting Orkla to launch a campaign against us, with help from the trade union, charging that we were trying to revoke their Swedish franchise. I immediately left St. Petersburg, Russia, where I had been visiting with Coke's new president, Doug Ivester, and flew to Oslo to set up, effectively, a war room.

Orkla, backed by the union drivers, took the drastic step of halting delivery of Coca-Cola within Norway until we relented in Sweden. Television news stories featured shots of store shelves being emptied of Coca-Cola products by union members. We tried to fill the gaps with other bottlers within Norway, but were making little headway. It was an attack on the integrity of the Coca-Cola franchise system and we could not back down. We were willing to pull out of Sweden and Norway if necessary. In this I had the full backing of Doug Ivester.

It just so happened that through my work with the Retail Research Council, I knew Stein Erik Hagan, who built one of the largest retail chains in Norway and was a purchaser not only of large volumes of Coca-Cola but also beer. "Leave it to me," Stein Erik told me. "I know exactly how to solve this."

He placed a large Coke order and when Orkla replied that it would not deliver, he told them not to bother delivering the beer either, which was a potentially devastating financial blow. It was as simple as that; in the short term the problem was solved and our products were returned to the shelves. It demonstrated not only the power of the retailer but also the power of good customer relations. Stein Erik saved the day. In the long term, we built our own bottling plants in Stockholm and Oslo, revoking the Orkla franchise and settling the lawsuit that ensued. We had successfully defended the integrity of the franchise system which later helped me as CEO when I finally completed consolidation of the German bottlers. They knew that my soft, collaborative side could be backed by a hard edge.

Meanwhile, business in the Eastern European countries including Hungary, Czechoslovakia, and even the smaller former Soviet republics such as Belarus expanded rapidly as we furiously built new plants and invested in existing factories.

Russia remained a much tougher market to crack. It started in 1990 with a McDonald's in Moscow and the big red Coca-Cola neon sign, but not much else. In Russia, the gray area between communism and capitalism lingered longer than it did in other countries. The economy had been so primitive under communism that some vending machines still dispensed Cokes into glass cups secured by a chain. Even paper cups were scarce under the communist system. The coin mechanisms on the vending machines often would be broken so attendants would stand there to take the customer's money. Each customer would drink Coke from the glass cup with the chain still attached. The next customer would drink from the same, unwashed cup. Clearly, we had a long way to go.

We struggled to secure a countertrade deal with Reynolds Aluminum for the production of can coil, with Coke guaranteeing to purchase $20 million a year of coil from the factory, but the Soviets could never quite grasp why they should have to pay Reynolds a licensing fee for the use of its technology. The Soviets spoke with great pride about how they had designed and manufactured the steel for their nation's space program and they could not fathom why they, great steel-makers that they were, should have to pay a company for its proprietary technology. The concept was completely foreign to them. They really had a hard time grasping the concept of capitalism: selling a product for a profit was foreign to them and there were few laws, government regulations, or agencies at that time that could even accommodate private investment.

In early 1991, Coke decided to build a $12 million company-owned bottling plant near Moscow, but it was illegal then for a foreign company to purchase land. Western investors normally worked in joint ventures with a Soviet partner, which would provide land as equity in the deal. We tried to lease land on our own, without a joint venture partner, the first time any Western company had attempted to do so. In fact, a law regulating the leasing of land was still being written and had not developed into anything concrete. Government officials also had no idea who owned the land: Was it the Soviet state, the Russian Republic, the Moscow City Council, or the state-owned farm that was then on the property?

Even if you could determine the rightful owner, what was the market price of the property when there was no market? And if you determined a value, there was no way to pay in convertible currency without 40 percent of the purchase price going directly to taxes.

We pushed on, despite all these obstacles, negotiating with the city of Moscow. The premise was, "We want to help you separate state from business." Then the entire structure of Moscow city government changed right before our eyes following a failed military coup in August 1991 that marked the end of the old Soviet Union. After the coup attempt, Moscow Mayor

Gavriil Popov destroyed the old communist system of managing the city. The decision-making process had been completely changed and we were no longer sure who was responsible for our building site. We were forced to forge relationships with the new government, the city's privatization committee, the Russian Federation Land Commission, President Boris Yelstin's staff, sanitation inspectors, and community action groups. We used eleven lawyers and went through fifteen revisions of the agreement before finally enduring a fourteen-hour meeting of the Moscow City Council.

The city priced the land, which was fifteen miles outside Moscow, at $5 million plus a lease payment each year, which made it as expensive as prime office space in Manhattan. It was an outrageous price and we walked out of the city council building without a deal.

Then Craig Cohon, whose father had engineered the first McDonald's in Moscow, managed to land a seat next to Mayor Popov on a ten-hour flight to the U.S. The mayor agreed that Coca-Cola would add value to the city and endorsed cutting the initial payment to $800,000 from the outrageous $5 million and extending the lowered lease payments over a 49-year period.

From October 16–25, we revised the lease agreement another ten times, deciding that the $800,000 initial payment would be allocated for scholarships at the International University of Moscow, and for medical supplies at a children's clinic. More negotiations ensued and we revised the lease agreement six more times, finally getting all the required signatures at 5 P.M. on December 17, the last minute of the last day before government closed down for the holidays.

We were not finished yet. The land lease could not go into

effect until the land registry was signed. Unfortunately, there was no land registry for Moscow or Russia. We spent the month of January helping the privatization committee create a registry. In March 1992, the Central Bank of Russia signed the land registry and the property officially belonged to Coca-Cola. We ordered the medical equipment and transferred money for the scholarships. Construction began. However, the saga was still not over. The city refused to honor the terms of the deal that required the city to pay for the connection of utilities. Coca-Cola had to spend an additional $500,000 or face even more delays.

The time, effort, and resources required to do even basic business transactions in the former Soviet Union were enormous. Yet the potential was also enormous.

Pepsi was initially outselling us 10 to 1 and was deeply entrenched with the communist government. As the central government weakened and formerly state-owned plants were privatized, Pepsi's advantage diminished. We swooped in to invest millions in ten factories where beer and cognac, in addition to soft drinks, were bottled. It was a roll of the dice because our legal team was writing some of the first private contracts in Russia, and even though the contracts were well-fashioned, there was no certainty of a court system that would enforce them in the event of a dispute. These were crazy deals as far as Pepsi was concerned. Yet they had failed to realize how quickly the power of the central government was failing. No longer did the central government have the money even to provide spare parts for the bottling plants. In the end, we recouped our investment on all but one of the plants. Our only loss occurred after the plant owner died of throat cancer and his son was debunked by the local mafia. Not surprisingly, the mafia refused to honor the contract.

I appointed Michael O'Neill, whom I had first met in Germany when our daughters attended the same international school, as Coke's new manager in Russia. A former trade representative for Ireland, he was stationed in the Soviet Union in the late 1970s and spoke Russian fluently.

When I lit the Coca-Cola sign at Pushkin Square, Michael was shivering on the roof of the building, making sure the electricity worked and that the sign did not fall on the crowd below.

Michael lived in a brick dacha built by German prisoners of war, in the forest about forty-five minutes outside Moscow. Stalin had once stayed there. During one of my visits to the dacha, I really started to get a sense of Russia. You were in this thick forest of birch trees. It was winter and it had snowed, but the sky had cleared and you could see the stars. There was the moon, a blanket of snow, the trees, and the stillness of the night. It was like a scene from *Dr. Zhivago*, whose author lies buried less than two miles away. Russia is a tough land, a hard land, but beautiful at the same time. You begin to understand the Russian soul, the depth of feeling for the earth.

Pamela and Cara would sometimes accompany me to Russia and one of their favorite spots was an open-air market where you could buy delicate rugs from the Caucasus at very low prices. Cara once bought two for $130 and promptly wrapped one of them around her to shield against the bitter Russian cold.

During one visit, Michael and I had been scheduled to go on a boat trip with a large group of business leaders. We arrived early so Michael suggested we drive a couple of kilometers away on Leningrad Highway to visit a cognac plant that we were using to bottle Coca-Cola products while the Moscow plant was under construction. The first batch of Fanta was just coming off the bottling line. The assistant manager proposed a toast, and we drank Fanta, mineral water, and cognac and ate bread and Russian sausages. He brought in three or four of the plant supervisors, who were all women, as was common in the old Soviet Union. With Michael acting as translator, we talked for hours about life in the new Russia and I was so enthralled we skipped the boat tour entirely.

One woman was already nostalgic for communism, primarily because she had fared well under the old system.

"Where do I send my kids in summer?" she asked. "It used to be that the state paid for children to go away for camp. What do I do now? My kids are on the street. I have to pay for my own vacation. The rents have gone up."

Conversely, a younger supervisor could clearly see the long-term benefits of market reform and the upside potential it promised. This was a common debate in Russia and was often delineated by age. It became an issue even inside Coca-Cola with older employees in Russia sometimes unable or unwilling to embrace the new system.

The frank discussion at the cognac plant was one of the most fascinating evenings of my life. Sadly, six months later, the manager of the plant was gunned down by the mafia.

"He was approached by the mafia to produce illegal cognac for them and he refused," Michael shared in an interview for this book. "They said they would ask a second time but would not ask a third. Unfortunately one morning leaving his apartment, he never got to his car."

It was not uncommon to occasionally hear gunfire on the

streets of Moscow as I discovered on a trip with Doug Ivester to tour the new bottling plant in Moscow. Doug had left the hotel about thirty minutes before me. As I was about to leave my room, I heard gunfire in the street. The Coca-Cola Company driver was caught in the crossfire of a mafia gun battle and was seriously wounded. Ivester had missed the bullets by a mere thirty minutes.

The more time I spent in Russia, the more deeply I became involved in its government, business, and culture. I was appointed to Russia's Foreign Affairs Advisory Council and we would meet every six months with the prime minister and the cabinet. The council was nominated by the PM and had most major international companies on it including the likes of British Petroleum and Mitsubishi, most represented by their CEOs. We discussed issues such as taxes, courts, and customs. That is where I built up many relationships and really started to understand Russia. I later followed Bob Strauss as chairman of the U.S.-Russia Business Council. I was never a true China hand, but I was becoming a Russia hand. The business connections led to cultural connections. I was named to the international board of directors of the Hermitage Museum in St. Petersburg, one of the largest and oldest museums in the world, founded in 1764 by Catherine the Great. As an amazing fringe benefit, I had the privilege of touring the ancient artwork in the basement, rarely displayed to the public; a truly priceless moment.

Coke's growing business in Russia made for some interesting trips to headquarters in Atlanta. We quickly learned that when the Russian bottlers were visiting, we had to empty the hotel minibars of all products except for Coca-Cola and beer. Otherwise, the Russians would empty the entire contents each day, taking the stash home with them in their suitcases, leaving a minibar bill that often exceeded the cost of the room.

Craig Cohon entertained a visiting delegation of Russians at a famous Atlanta nude-dancing establishment, the Gold Club, submitting an expense account to the company for several thousand dollars, a code of conduct violation which outraged the head of internal auditing. He wanted Craig to be fired. We worked it out so that Craig would pay the bill out of his own pocket. Craig, who is now vice chairman of Cirque du Soleil, framed the receipt and to this day it hangs on the wall in a bathroom at his home.

On a separate visit to Atlanta, the mayor of St. Petersburg, Anatoly Sobchak, purchased Coca-Cola underwear at the company gift shop. In typical Russian fashion, he rolled down his trousers during a meeting and proudly displayed the new boxer shorts.

We had agreed to build a bottling plant in St. Petersburg, with a young, steely-eyed former KGB agent named Vladimir Putin handling the negotiations as head of the city's Foreign Economic Relations Department.

Coca-Cola was soon gaining on Pepsi, which never seemed to realize what had hit them.

"They were sleeping," Michael said of our competitors in blue. Pepsi lost its 10 to 1 advantage and by 1994, Coca-Cola gained the lead, which it retains to this day.

Coca-Cola helped deliver capitalism to Russia and Eastern Europe. We discovered citizens hungry to learn how a successful company works, realizing they had been educated in the past using theoretical concepts which ultimately failed.

In the early years after the Wall fell, smaller foreign companies lacked the resources and patience to participate in this transformation. Coca-Cola was large enough to take the risk, breaking ground for others to follow. Capitalism provided the foundation not only for new business enterprises but for new nations.

I am a firm believer that capitalism is the most potent form of foreign assistance. We should consider whether some of the many billions governments now devote to social development projects would be better spent on tax credits to encourage companies to invest in poor countries. Unlike social development projects, business investment has a larger multiplier effect and usually leads to even larger, more profitable companies that follow, literally freeing people from poverty.

Along with the rapid changes taking place in Eastern Europe came another momentous event: Nelson Mandela was released from prison on February 11, 1990, having spent twenty-seven years behind bars. The days of South African apartheid were clearly numbered.

Carl Ware, who by 1991 was working for me as deputy group president overseeing Africa, set up a luncheon in Johannesburg with three members of the African National Congress: Mandela, Thabo Mbeki, and Yusuf Surtee. I knew Yusuf from my time in Johannesburg. Because I was tall, I required tailored suits and Yusuf was my tailor, which was his day job. Little did we know that this charming merchant was also working with the ANC. Eventually, he popped up as one of the key people helping Mandela.

In this, my first meeting with Mandela, I felt the need to subtly mention that I had opposed apartheid. As I started telling the story of my college activism, Mandela put his hand on my forearm and, speaking slowly and deliberately, said "Mr. Isdell, don't worry. We know all about you." Mandela could have let me continue with my uncomfortable spiel but instead displayed a real sense of empathy.

Yusuf, who had obviously briefed Mandela about me, beamed. I felt more confident than ever about the future of South Africa and Coca-Cola's role there.

In October 1993, I was extremely honored to present Mandela with the first J. William Fulbright Prize for International Understanding, a $50,000 award funded by the Coca-Cola Company. It was a powerful and emotional event.

Presenting the award, I recalled how my fellow college students and I had demonstrated for Mandela's release: "Though it was, in fact, thirty years ago, I have very vivid memories that somewhat overwhelm me today, memories rendered indelibly on the impressionable mind of a young, red-headed Irishman, who was inspired by the courage of those who were brave enough to risk their lives to end organized injustice in South Africa."

Mandela spoke about South Africa's first democratic elections scheduled for 1994: "Incredible as it may sound, at the age of seventy-five I have never, ever participated in a general election," he said. "The prospect of finally receiving the opportunity to participate is one that is indeed very exciting. It will be the culmination of decades of political struggle and personally a goal for which I have striven throughout these years."

Mandela not only voted in that election, he was elected president of South Africa, a truly historic milestone.

Mandela was succeeded by Mbeki. Carl then was in charge of Coke in Africa. I had a new challenge, this one involving nearly a billion people.

Six

GOING BACK TO INDIA

C oca-Cola left South Africa over apartheid. In the Middle East, we were ejected for selling our products in Israel. In India, we departed for an entirely different reason: the secret formula.

In 1977 a newly elected Indian government demanded that we partner with an Indian company and disclose the secret formula, which we refused to do. Then we packed our bags and left the world's second most populous country. For those who believe the secret formula is nothing more than a marketing myth, let India be a lesson. In defense of our secret formula, we walked away from a market of a billion people, as did IBM after refusing to reveal its source code.

India began liberalizing its economy in the early 1990s under Manmohan Singh, then the finance minister and now the prime minister. Coke had the opportunity to return.

As the reentry slowly progressed under John Hunter, I gained India as part of my territory in 1993, although I lost Africa to

Carl Ware. I liked and respected Carl but was very unhappy about this decision because of my lifelong ties to Africa. Also, without Africa, the sales volume in my group was diminished by half since sales in the Indian market were minuscule at the time. Once again, I was given a turnaround market.

It was a blow and I considered leaving the company for the first time since that night in Germany when Heinz Wiezorek and I vowed to resign. The difference now was that I would soon turn fifty and retirement was within reach. I was going to have to live with it. I told Pamela, "I'm going to build what I have into something as big as what I used to have. I'll show them just what I can do." I also was reassured by Don Keough and John Hunter that the move was in no way performance related but situational and that my future was still bright.

India proved to be a very interesting, enjoyable, and challenging assignment. It was equally the most fascinating country I've ever worked in and the most frustrating. The images in my memory of India are stunning. Pamela and I will never forget the Beating of the Retreat in Delhi, a military ceremony dating back to the 1600s. It's theater like you've never seen, held each year in January, in front of the Parliament Building. As the sun sets, spotlights illuminate the Camel Corps. The best military bands play and soldiers march past the reviewing stand. There are soldiers playing bagpipes, wearing kilts. As a bugler sounds the call for retreat, the Indian flags are slowly lowered and the bands march away. Close your eyes and you will believe the British raj never left.

When I assumed responsibility for India, Coke's reentry was at a very tentative stage. Coca-Cola, under Hunter's direction, had formed a joint venture with Rajan Pillai, who had gained

At age three in Belfast with my parents, Edward and Margaret. My father, a fingerprint specialist with the Royal Ulster Constabulary and an avid rugby player, longed to leave Northern Ireland and to ensure that I received a college education.

With my dog, Bunty, in Northern Ireland.

Playing rugby (center) for the University of Cape Town. Rugby has always been a major part of my life and taught me many lessons that were useful in the rough-and-tumble world of business.

The most important meeting of my life. Pamela and I met in
Lusaka, Zambia, and were married there on January 10, 1970.
We have been married for more than 41 years.

Conquering Pepsi in the Philippines. Jesus Celdran, nicknamed King King, was crucial to Coke's turnaround in the Philippines. We are pictured here in Leyte in front of the monument to General Douglas MacArthur.

In front of the Coca-Cola sign in Moscow's Pushkin Square in late 1989, shortly after the Berlin Wall fell and the first McDonald's opened in Russia. It was the first commercial sign in Moscow, a harbinger of capitalism.

With Muhtar Kent (center) and Coca-Cola CEO and Chairman Roberto Goizueta, as we moved rapidly into Eastern Europe following the fall of the Berlin Wall.

With Jay Raja at the Taj Mahal in India. Jay was Coke's point man during the reentry into India.

Awarding the Fulbright Prize to South African President Nelson Mandela in 1993.

Greeting Coca-Cola employees at the Atlanta headquarters in May 2004, when my appointment as CEO and Chairman was announced.

Pamela and me with Prince Charles. I would later have a disagreement with the prince over a nonprofit merger, which knocked me off the royal Christmas card list.

A second happy retirement. In Barbados, after retiring for the second time, with Pamela, our daughter, Cara, son-in-law, Zak Lee, and grandson, Rory.

control of Indian-based cookie-maker Britannia Biscuits. Pillai had also purchased the Asian operations of RJR Nabisco, with the help of a group of investors, including RJR's former CEO, F. Ross Johnson, a friend of Don Keough's.

The idea was for Pillai to move his Singapore-based snack-food plant to a new factory in India, which would also produce Coke concentrate. Celebrating the joint venture, Pillai held a lavish party at his home in Mumbai, complete with fire-eaters and snake charmers, all the top film stars, and other members of the Indian glitterati. As I watched all this, it struck me as out of sync with the conservative image of the Coca-Cola Company. I smelled a bit of a rat. It turned out that Pillai was expensing the party through the joint venture. We were paying for this outrageous entertainment.

Soon after, I started negotiating to sever our relationship with Pillai. At the same time, Pillai's business empire was collapsing and he was indicted in Singapore for fraud. In response, he fled to India where he lived as a fugitive, moving from hotel to hotel to avoid arrest. I later ran into Pillai at the Oberoi Hotel in Delhi where, although a wanted man, he approached me as an old friend, and we exchanged warm greetings. He was, as the Irish saying goes, a likeable rogue. Sadly, he died in an Indian jail in 1995 of complications from cirrhosis of the liver.

Our attention then shifted to Parle Beverages, which controlled 60 percent of the Indian soft drink market, and had developed the wildly successful spicy cola, Thums Up, after Coke's exit from India in 1977.

Jay Raja, my former group marketing manager who was leading the reentry efforts on the ground in India, was at first reluctant to talk to Parle, believing it had been behind Coke's ejection from India in the first place. Parle had also opposed the Indian government's 1992 decision to allow Coke to return. Jay suspected that Parle was also discussing a joint venture with Pepsi.

At the same time, key Parle bottlers were approaching Jay about defecting to Coca-Cola,

Parle was owned by two brothers, Ramesh and Prakash Chauhan, who were quickly realizing that they would not be able to effectively compete with giants Coke and Pepsi. "When elephants fight, the grass gets trampled!" Ramesh told Jay.

Parle was not an ideal partner for Coke; its bottling plants were in dire need of upgrades. Yet Parle's nationwide system would provide Coke with a speedy entry back into a potentially huge market, and Coke would instantly gain 60 percent of the Indian soft drink market, a lead that would surely grow once we reintroduced Coke products.

We made an offer to purchase Parle for $32 million, which seems a grand bargain given the size of the country and Parle's huge market lead. Yet India's soft drink market was tiny then. "The total amount of soft drinks sold in India was about the amount sold in the city of Atlanta back then," recalled John Heaton, my executive assistant who was in charge of executing the deal. "Many people in India just didn't have any money to buy soft drinks. They drank tea, coffee, milk, and roadside fruit juice."

Annual soft drink consumption in India at the time averaged three bottles a person, Heaton said. You will recall that when I left the Philippines in 1984, the per capita consumption was 134 bottles per year. That illustrates how poor India really was and also how poorly soft drinks had been marketed, but also its enormous upside potential.

We also offered the Chauhan brothers the bottling franchises in Mumbai and part of Delhi, a lucrative proposition. We haggled over the price, eventually settling on $40 million.

Prakash was willing to sell but his older brother Ramesh had cold feet, reluctant to relinquish the title of India's soft drink king; his picture frequently graced the cover of magazines. Ramesh finally relented, but not happily. He and his wife sobbed at the contract signing in Atlanta.

The Chauhans graciously hosted a party at their home in Mumbai and unfortunately I fell ill on the return flight, immediately taking an antibiotic that I had with me for just this type of emergency. Upon arriving in Atlanta, I instructed my driver to take me directly to Piedmont Hospital. Doctors told me it was an amoebic infection called Shigella, not from the food at the party but from earlier handshakes, which is the main means of transmission, and I was out of commission for a week.

The Chauhan's astrologer told them the closing had to take place at 3 P.M. on a Saturday afternoon. It was scheduled for November 11, 1993. John Heaton and Jay handled it while I was upstairs working in my office. The usual haggling made it likely that the astrologers would be sorely disappointed. As midnight approached, John suggested that the parties sign one of the shorter documents and complete the remainder the following day.

We had captured a 60 percent market share, a major coup. India was a tough market, however, where media-fueled controversies cropped up continuously, sometimes over the smallest of matters.

We celebrated our first franchise bottler in India in late October 1993 in Agra, home of the Taj Mahal. It was a huge event, covered by international media. "Neville, we have a problem," one of Coke's public relations executives told me. A reporter had spotted a young boy working on the bottling line. The reporter wanted to write a story that Coke was using child labor upon its return to India. We assured the reporter that there was no child labor and we rushed to track down the boy in question. It turns out he was not a worker but the son of a plant employee, proudly inspecting the assembly line in a white lab coat. It was one of those moments when I thought everything was going to fall off a cliff: from pride in reentering India to absolute disaster over child labor.

The headaches were well worth it, although it took time. Coke's sales volume in India jumped 50 percent in the first two years and captured almost two-thirds of the market. Despite that success, Jay Raja resigned from the company in 1995, after being hammered for two years from both sides: Indian media accused him of trying to kill a national icon, Thums Up, to promote Coke and Fanta, while Coca-Cola executives at North Avenue, including Douglas Daft who was then in charge of Asia, made the opposite charge. Sergio Zyman, the father of New Coke who resigned after the 1985 debacle and was rehired in 1993 as the company's chief marketing officer, was, in fact, lukewarm about Thums Up. Many executives, Jay and myself included, believed it would be disastrous to kill Thums Up. Even Don Keough, then the company president, questioned at the time of the purchase whether we should keep Thums Up. Wouldn't that mean having two colas in the Indian market? I replied that Thums Up was not a cola but a pepper drink, similar to Dr. Pepper. Don asked me what the Indian customers believed Thums Up to be. Some customers believed it was a cola,

I had to admit, but they were wrong, and there was no "cola" in the brand name. Don smiled and agreed that we should keep Thums Up. Even to this day, Thums Up is the top cola in India.

The Chauhan brothers contributed further to Jay's headaches. They were minority owners of Gujarat Bottling Company, a Coke bottler, which sold its assets to Pepsi. So Jay was confronted with a Coke bottler working out of a Pepsi-owned bottling plant. Coke sued and won a restraining order barring GBC from bottling Pepsi products, a move that Jay believed kept Pepsi from conducting similar raids on other Coke bottlers in India. Yet Daft scolded him for "unnecessarily" damaging relations with the Chauhan brothers.

Daft also pushed Jay to build a large-scale consolidated bottling system in India. "I will show you what a world class system looks like by replicating China in India," Jay recalls Daft as saying. Daft's thinking was correct in the long term. The Indian market was so price competitive, given the country's extreme poverty, that it would only turn a profit if the bottling system was extremely efficient and low cost.

Yet Jay argued, correctly, that India's infrastructure was not yet prepared to handle a large company-owned bottling system and that it would be better to work with the franchised bottlers to improve their plants. Also, Jay worried that abandoning the Indian bottlers would be a violation of the company's pledge to the Indian government to support an indigenous, independent industry.

Meanwhile Zyman blocked Jay's efforts to sign a young cricket star, Sachin Tendulkar, as a Coke spokesperson, arguing that it would be a waste of money. Pepsi signed Tendulkar instead and he turned out to be one of the best cricket players of all time. In early 2011, Coke signed him, although he is now nearing the end of his career.

Jay's resignation was unfortunate. He was a valuable leader and proved to be correct on many crucial points, while laying the foundation for a market that would eventually become lucrative for Coke. Sales in India grew steadily over the years and today it is one of Coke's fastest-growing markets, holding four of the top five brands: Thums Up, Limca, Sprite, and Fanta. Still, it was not until 2009 that Coke finally made a profit in India.

At the time of Jay's departure, I was no longer in charge of India. Doug Ivester had by then been named company president, succeeding Don Keough, who retired as Robert Goizeuta ushered in a new, younger generation of executives, clearly setting up Ivester as his successor. Ivester's promotion effectively ended John Hunter's ascension. Yet John, who had been Keough's choice to be president, stayed on as head of international. In 1995, Ivester took Europe out of Hunter's portfolio and gave it to me. This fractured my relationship with Hunter, who I had happily worked both for and with. He had engineered the Philippines deal that had been so pivotal to my career. John believed I had lobbied for Europe, which was not the case. The new president asked me to run Europe and I accepted. It was as simple as that yet it did mean that I was effectively John's peer, reporting directly to Ivester. Together with Jack Stahl, the U.S. president, we were the three operating heads. John stayed on for another year but it was terribly awkward. I would attend the monthly meetings John had with his direct reports, but I was not working for him. He didn't like that at all. "I hope we can get past this," I said once to John. "I don't think we ever can," was his reply. Time heals, of course, and John and I are now good friends again, occasionally having dinner and socializing together. He would have been a strong company leader, but that was not to be.

With Europe now part of my territory, I had, by the mid-1990s, reached a very high-profile position at Coca-Cola. My territory generated a third of the company's profits.

It was in this job that I soon had my own Sergio Zyman stories to tell. During a meeting in Madrid, Gavin Darby, who ran Northwest Europe, made a presentation before Ivester, the company president, and other executives from Atlanta. Gavin's presentation went on a bit too long. Sergio started yawning and eventually lay on the floor, pretending to be asleep. I looked at Ivester but he said nothing. This is the license that Sergio had. He was very close not only to Ivester, who had no background in marketing and was in line to be the next CEO, but also to Roberto. Sergio was Mexican, and Roberto, Cuban. They spoke Spanish to each other at company functions.

I asked to see Ivester after the meeting and we went for a walk where I flatly told him that Sergio's behavior was unacceptable. "The fleas come with the dog," Doug replied. "He's a great dog. We're just going to accept the fleas."

Sergio also clashed with Weldon Johnson, who ran Latin America. Sergio pushed to have him removed. After Weldon left the company, a triumphant Sergio walked into my office and asked me if I had a nickel. I fished one out of my pocket.

"This is going to be the best advice you'll ever get for a nickel," Sergio told me. "Resign now. You're next after Weldon." For the first time, I felt uncomfortable in the executive suites of the Coca-Cola Company, and began thinking of how I could get out.

The CEO's position was clearly not in the cards for me. At lunch one day in the North Avenue dining room, Roberto told me he planned to remain as Chairman and CEO for a long time. Eventually Ivester would take over as CEO and Roberto would stay on indefinitely as chairman, a part-time position that would have suited Roberto since he usually arrived at work around 8 A.M. each day and went home around 4 in the afternoon. He was a strategist and a delegator. As part of this strategy, Roberto planned to beef up the duties and pay of the group presidents, of which I was one, giving them a larger role in running the company. However, I would still be part of a corporate bureaucracy, a situation in which I never really flourished. While not politically inept, I was politically uncomfortable, and it sometimes showed. I wanted to run my own company, having always performed the best in situations, such as the Philippines, where I was in charge.

At the same time, I began considering my retirement—which I planned for a time between my fifty-fifth and fifty-eighth birthdays—with three goals in mind: to be physically active, stay intellectually engaged, and spend time with Pamela.

I discussed my future with Roberto and Doug Ivester, telling them that in the last few years of my working career, I wanted to run a publicly traded company. Given that I could retire at fifty-five and cash in all my restricted stock and stock options, this would be financially attractive. Roberto and Doug decided to create a company for me, Coca-Cola Beverages, which would be formed by consolidating the bottlers in Europe and would be traded on the London Stock Exchange. It was just in time. Soon afterward, the ages at which restricted stock options could be exercised was raised to fifty-eight.

As we worked out the details for CCB, it became increasingly obvious that Roberto was ill. A chain smoker, Roberto never went to the doctor for checkups. Over time, we'd begun to notice that he'd become forgetful, complaining at monthly management meetings, that we, the senior managers, had failed to inform him of key actions and events, when clearly we had. Doug Ivester convened an important meeting of top executives, telling us, "Roberto is ill. You've all seen it. We're going to have to help him, but in effect, we're going to have to run the company."

About nine months later, on October 18, 1997, Roberto died of complications from lung cancer. He was only sixty-five. I saw Roberto at Emory University Hospital three days before he died. "Take care of my company," he told me. Roberto had an incredible seventeen-year tenure as Chairman and CEO, increasing the company's market value from $4 billion to $150 billion. In 1996 alone, stockholders saw a forty-six percent return. Only today has the company's market value matched its peak under Roberto's leadership. As expected, the board picked Ivester as the new Chairman and CEO.

That fall, I prepared to leave for London, hoping to officially wrap up my duties in Atlanta by the end of 1997. Yet it took until February for Ivester to name my replacement. I was technically leaving Coca-Cola since CCB would be a separate company. As I was preparing to walk out the doors of North Avenue, the secretaries discovered that there had been no farewell planned for me by the Coca-Cola Company, so they hastily prepared a small get together. Ivester was not there. And I never received a formal farewell from the Coca-Cola Company.

In London we rented a charming two-bedroom flat. Pamela and I decided that there would be no need to move our entire

household again—as we had so many times before—since we
believed this would be the final chapter of my career. We also
knew this was going to be a short assignment, probably no
more than three or four years. So Pamela would stay put in Atlanta and would visit me in London when I was there. Since I
was the CEO of the new company, I controlled my own travel
schedule and could be in London whenever it was convenient
for her. Cara was then a student at the University of South
Carolina, a true Southern girl after all her world travels.

CCB was a fun job from day one. I was away from an increasingly toxic atmosphere at North Avenue, on my own in London.
Financially, I was secure for life, with my Coca-Cola stock
options and pension. I was not only running my own company
but creating it as well.

My task was to take the European business of the Australian-
based bottler, Coca-Cola Amatil, combine it with Coca-Cola's
Italian bottling business, and float it as a new company on the
London Stock Exchange. In February 1998, I started working
alone out of my hotel room in London, assembling a team. I
hired Craig Owens, who was then heading the company-owned
bottler in France, as chief financial officer. Craig is now CFO of
Campbell Soup Company. John Culhane moved from Atlanta
to become chief legal counsel. I recruited Cynthia McCague,
then working in London for Coke, to be human resources director and Gavin Bell to handle investor relations. We worked in
a one-room office, slowly building up to the stock float. The
proceeds from the stock issue would go to Coca-Cola Amatil,
so Craig and I had long discussions with the Amatil executives
about their expectations for the initial stock price. Craig,
Gavin, and I toured Europe and the U.S., briefing investment

houses on the stock and gauging interest. Anyone who has ever done an IPO knows that this is an exhausting and boring process: eighty-nine meetings in three weeks, repeating the same presentation over and over again. Investors apparently liked our management team and they liked having a new Coca-Cola company entity. We were thirteen times oversubscribed for the stock and in June 1998, we gathered with the investment bankers to set an opening price. In fact, I had made a mistake in agreeing to a wide price band, not believing that the top of the band would attract so many investors. Amatil execs, on the phone in Sydney, were so enthused about the oversubscription that they wanted to offer the stock at a price even higher than the band we had established, making the shares more expensive and at the same time, adding pressure on me, the founding CEO, to deliver earnings results to justify the inflated price.

I was taken aside by the lead investment banker, an aristocratic Englishman who told me I really did not understand how it all worked. "This is your first IPO, is it not?" he asked. "Well, the sellers and the bankers set the price. You have no say in this."

My reply was blunt. "Who are you going to get to run the company?" I asked. "If you go outside the band, I'm not going to run it." My job was to maximize return for Amatil, but not beyond the price range upon which we had previously agreed. They tried to push me and I pushed back. I won the battle. On July 13, 1998, the stock debuted on the high end of the band, with a market value of $2.72 billion.

Six weeks after the successful and lofty stock float, Russia suffered a severe financial crisis, triggered by the earlier Asian crisis that had suppressed demand for commodities such as oil, a crucial export for the Russian economy. Fortunately, CCB had no business in Russia, but the crisis there dampened stock prices worldwide. CCB stock dropped and our new investors were very unhappy. Friends of mine who had purchased stock lost money. Even when I left CCB in 2001, the stock price had not recovered to its initial offering price. In addition to the Russian economic meltdown, Coke sales were hurt by a contamination scare in Belgium in 1999. Belgium was not a CCB bottler and the scare turned out to be just that, with no contamination ever proven. Yet Ivester did not manage the controversy well, his career was damaged and, temporarily, sales and profits in Europe decreased.

All along, CCB was seen as a way to consolidate Europe into a single bottler. The most obvious target for a merger was Coca-Cola Hellenic, based out of Athens and owned by the Leventis family. The family bought the Greek bottling franchise from Coca-Cola in the 1970s and turned it around. They still owned Nigeria and also had plants in Ireland, Russia, Romania, Bulgaria, and other parts of Eastern Europe.

Andrew David ran many of the family businesses including the bottling operations. It was he whom I had confronted in Nigeria over subpar bottling plant conditions, and with whom I had subsequently become close friends. Andrew had an affinity for Ireland, having attended Trinity College, and was an avid rugby fan. So we forged a strong relationship over the years.

We agreed that HBC and Hellenic would merge and I would run the joint company. We would have to move the stock listing to Greece, otherwise it would be seen as a sale rather than a merger, and the Leventis family would be subject to heavy taxes. The merger was completed in August 2000, creating a new company called Coca-Cola Hellenic Bottling Co., one of the largest

Coke bottlers in the world. The Leventis family received about 23 percent of the stock in the new company. Coca-Cola still owns 24 percent of CCHBC. Sadly, Andrew David died shortly after the merger. His brother, George, who took over as chairman, felt that I had out-negotiated Andrew. I don't believe I had, but George and I were never close.

The other piece of the European consolidation puzzle was Coca-Cola Enterprises, the Atlanta-based bottler which owned the franchise in Great Britain. Early in the life of CCHBC, I met with Summerfield Johnson, then CEO of Coca-Cola Enterprises, at Andrew David's flat in London and we held a long discussion. Summerfield seemed interested in some sort of merger but later phoned me to say the timing was not right. The deal was never consummated.

Hungary was one particularly tough challenge, where a price war raged between Coke and Pepsi. Each time Pepsi dropped prices, the Hungarian bottler felt compelled to match it; a game of chicken. My experience in the Philippines kicked in and I assured the Hungarian management that Pepsi was hurting as badly as Coke was and that Pepsi was lowering prices only with the help of an unsustainable subsidy from the parent company. "We're going to lead a price increase," I told the Hungarians. We raised prices and Coke sales were down for about three weeks before Pepsi followed suit and matched the increase. It was a nervous three weeks for me.

Meanwhile, we realized we had to convince Coca-Cola to lower concentrate prices, not an easy task.

Near the end of his life, Roberto Goizueta had announced to Wall Street that Coca-Cola had a new stream of revenue: the buying and selling of bottlers. We were buying bottlers, upgrading them, and selling them to investors for top dollar. For example, the East European bottlers we had invested in were sold to Coca-Cola Amatil, arguably for too much money but with a gain for the Coca-Cola Company. Wall Street loved it and in July 1998 Coke stock hit an all-time high of $88 per share. However, there was a problem: When a company such as Coca-Cola Amatil bought a bottler at top dollar, it would have to achieve a much higher profit margin to recoup its investment. That would require raising prices on its products. Raising prices temporarily helped Coca-Cola as well because it could then charge more for concentrate.

Eventually, though, that game comes to an end as bottlers can no longer raise prices without losing market share. And the game did come to an end, in Hungary and other Eastern European countries in late 1998.

In 2000, I flew to Atlanta with Andrew David, chairman of CCHBC, to meet with Douglas Daft who was the new CEO, following Doug Ivester's short-lived tenure. I made a pitch for lowering concentrate prices for Hungary as a way to give the bottler a chance to get back on its feet. Jack Stahl, the company's new president under Daft, at first balked at the request.

"The Coca-Cola Company is never, ever going to do that," Jack said.

"Fine," I said. "But you are going to have a bankrupt bottler on your hands."

Daft, to his credit, realized the old model had been pushed too far and agreed to lower concentrate prices, which hurt profits, Coke's stock price, and Daft's career. Although it was largely a problem he inherited, he had the courage to do the right thing.

I promised Pamela that I would retire at age fifty-eight, and

I could see clearly that the relationship with George David, board chairman of the new company, CCHBC, after his brother's death, would be strained. So I announced that I would leave CCHBC at the end of 2001. I had done what I wanted to do: create a public company and consolidated a huge part of Europe. Also, CCHBC was in discussions at the time to purchase the Russian bottler from Coca-Cola. Irial Finan, my successor, closed the deal in 2002 for $100 million. A year earlier, I had walked away from negotiations when Coke's bottom line price was $500 million. Today, the Russian bottler is probably worth $1 billion, making it the best deal I was ever involved in, and a bad one for the Coca-Cola Company.

Pamela and I had purchased a house in Barbados and now had all the pieces in place for retirement: winter in Barbados, summer in France, and spring in Atlanta where the azaleas are in bloom and the Masters Golf Tournament is nearby.

After leaving CCHBC, I dabbled in real estate development in Barbados and started a small investment company. I became the majority shareholder of a company called Elstat, which makes energy-saving thermostats for commercial coolers. These are now widely used in the Coca-Cola network and I had to place my shares of Elstat into a blind trust when I returned to Coke as Chairman and CEO. Of course, I tried to sharpen my golf game in retirement, and with the lower stress of day-to-day living lost fifteen pounds. And Pamela and I traveled, visiting such places as Tahiti, New Zealand, and, as always, Africa. Coca-Cola was rarely on my mind.

In August 2003, I got a call from a friend and former Coke bottler now working as a consultant. He had been among those sitting in the pew with us that unforgettable Sunday morning in Poland's St. Brigid's Church when we had celebrated the opening of the first Coke plant in Eastern Europe. "Neville, a number of us have got together and we're going to start lobbying for Daft to go and for you to come back and run the Coca-Cola Company," the consultant said. Earnings were down and Coca-Cola stock had dropped to less than half its 1998 peak. More important, morale was really bad. Daft, in a way, seemed to have lost interest in the job. He would say to people, "I'm just going to do whatever I can to get fired." It would sound as if he were joking, but there was some truth in it. Doug was obviously exhausted.

I gave the consultant a Shermanesque response. "I'm not going to do it," I told him. "I'm happily retired. My wife loves having me around. You're going down a blind alley." I added that he had no mandate from me to put my name forward.

The behind-the-scenes movement to draft me did not abate, and I received other calls from people in the system. I gave them the same answer: "I am definitely not interested." The following spring came *the call* from Don Keough. This time, it was serious.

Seven

AT THE HELM OF COCA-COLA

After Roberto Goizueta's death, Coca-Cola began to falter. For so many years, the company had been blessed with two great leaders: Goizueta and Don Keough. However, Roberto had died and Don had retired. Doug Ivester, the company's first leader in the post–Goizueta-Keough era, did not last long. He resigned as Chairman and CEO after slightly more than two years. Daft survived for more than four years, although frankly, he probably should have left earlier. I believe he stayed as long as he did, in part, because the board did not want to face the grim reality that two successive choices for the top job had failed to get the company back on track.

In all fairness, Roberto's performance was not sustainable, particularly given the changes in the global economy. He pushed us all to the absolute limit. He would go to Wall Street and say, "We are going to be able to deliver 15 percent growth in earnings per share." Those of us on the front lines thought that 11 or 12 percent were more realistic numbers and would attempt to tell Roberto as such. "Fine," Roberto would reply. "Wall Street is expecting 15 percent." A company and its executives can only do that for so long, particularly when world events go against you as they did in the second half of 1998.

Gary Fayard, Coke's current chief financial officer who was then controller, remembers the year well. "In the first half of 1998, the company grew its volume 12 percent," Gary recalled. "We had a huge analysts meeting in Atlanta in May. The analysts were asking when we were going to take our earnings and growth targets up. I'm sitting in the back of the Goizueta Auditorium reading the *Financial Times* and it says, 'Asian Flu, Russia Devolving, Argentine Meltdown.' The whole world is going to hell except the U.S. Yet our volume was still skyrocketing. We were hiring people left and right. The bottlers were building plants, borrowing money, just growing everywhere."

It did not take long, however, for the economic turmoil to hit Coca-Cola's bottom line.

"In the second half of 1998, our volume increase went from 12 percent to zero," Gary remembered. "Overnight, the world stopped. Our business stopped. But you've hired so many people; the bottlers have so much debt from building plants and making acquisitions. The bottlers are in a very bad position. The company is bloated with overhead."

Ivester had launched a project in 1999, later executed by Daft, named the Strategic Organizational Alignment, a code name for mass layoffs, which were unheard of at Coke, where a job had almost always meant a job for life. Coke fired more than five thousand people, deeply shaking the company.

"The layoffs killed us," Gary recalled. "We lost momentum. We lost morale. That is where we really started losing our way."

The company indeed needed to shed costs. Yet the firings were not implemented effectively. It was not a Strategic Organizational Alignment; it was a head-cutting exercise. Many of the heads that were cut were heads that had special skills and deep business knowledge. In some instances, the fired employees set up consultancies and provided their skills back to Coke at a higher cost. I had met with Daft in January 2000 at his request to outline the process I had used to establish CCHBC, the merger of Coca-Cola Beverages with Hellenic. While it was not a perfect process, it was based on first defining what work needed to be undertaken, thereby identifying where there was duplication and redundancy. Once a new organization structure was identified we only then filled the boxes. Where we had two or more people qualified for the same position, we used our evaluation process to select the right person. This meant a better, leaner structure and the placement and retention of the best people. Doug reacted favorably but never followed up. I wish he had for events as they unfolded may have been different.

When I took over as Chairman and CEO, there was still an atmosphere of fear and disaffection at Coca-Cola. Clearly, I had my work cut out for me. Yet, there was one immediate fire that I had to extinguish quickly on my first official day in office, June 1, 2004. It was so important that I was actually not in the office that day or even in Atlanta. I was in Chicago at the headquarters of Coke's largest fountain client, McDonald's.

Steve Heyer, Coke's president who had been the only internal candidate for Chairman and CEO, had deeply offended McDonald's by gloating over a new contract with Subway, insinuating that Subway got better terms. It wasn't true, but it came across that way and we had reliable information that McDonald's was holding discussions with Pepsi about selling some of their non-cola brands. If a single McDonald's had dispensed a Pepsi product, that likely would have damaged my newly resurrected career. It would have been an unprecedented failure.

I met with Charlie Bell, the CEO of McDonald's, and looking him straight in the eye, told him flatly, "I will fix the problem." Bell understood what I meant: Heyer would soon be leaving the company. Meanwhile, we conducted a complete audit to make sure we weren't overcharging McDonald's, and ended up refunding some money in a few areas, although there were no major overcharges. I later bolstered the McDonald's relationship further by changing management, naming Jerry Wilson to head the account. He did a superb job and was followed by Roberto's son, Javier Goizueta. Javier had suffered somewhat from the fact that within the company, people had tended to view him as the former chairman's son, overlooking his real talent as a manager. He ended up performing admirably and has ensured that the vital relationship with McDonald's remains strong. You have to earn your relationship with your customers each and every day, and my visit that day to McDonald's was intended to send that message. If you take a customer for granted, you do so at your own peril.

From Chicago I then flew to the West Coast to meet with Peter Ueberroth, a Coke board member and head of the audit committee, to seek his advice and counsel. Peter, who successfully ran the Los Angeles Olympics, headed the well-named Contrarian Group, which has helped many successful companies. Although I didn't know Ueberroth well, I had watched him over the years when I presented to the Coke board and he was always one of those who asked tough, insightful questions. I had many difficult issues to face and throughout my tenure he was someone I trusted totally and was always able to turn to for sound analysis and advice, as of course was my mentor, Don Keough.

It is normal that the first one hundred days mark the clear enunciation of strategy and while I made a number of moves internally through major appointments, I declared that I would not speak to the media or the analysts during that period. I did not want to make declarations based on preconceived ideas I'd developed in Barbados as I watched events unfold, but wanted to learn more by traveling around the world visiting our operations and meeting with employees, customers, and other key individuals with whom the company had relationships.

I had decided that I was not going to immediately have a president. Frankly, I simply did not believe that there was anyone in the company at the time who was qualified for the job, which illustrates how badly flawed Coca-Cola's succession management had been. It does no good to have a second in command unless that person has the potential to run the company. Daft had one vice chairman and two presidents during his tenure. Yet Coca-Cola still languished and the board, in hiring me out of retirement, was forced to reach outside the company for a new Chairman and CEO.

Some people advised me to get rid of Heyer right away and clearly I agreed he did not have the right skills to be president. I wanted to ease him out quietly. I thought that approach was better for the organization, and I also wanted to travel around the world for the first few months to get a feel for the pulse of the business. I needed someone at headquarters to maintain the status quo until I could fully understand what needed to be done. Heyer knew his days at Coke were numbered, and during my first week on the job he walked into my office and handed me a document which he said had been approved by Daft. The document stated that Heyer would receive $26 million in severance pay for leaving the company.

It was a shock to me and it was a shock to the Coke board of directors. Clearly, Daft had the authority to approve the contract, but you would think that given the order of magnitude, the board would have been told about it. Yet they hadn't, which was a shock to all.

I consulted with board members Peter Ueberroth and Cathie Black, head of the Comp Committee and later (briefly) chancellor of the New York City school system, to work our way through it. Heyer believed he had an ironclad commitment and we decided to meet it, as hard as that was to accept. The last thing we needed was another lawsuit on our hands.

I first met Heyer during my first retirement when as an international advisor to the company. I was asked to help Heyer with the customers in Europe with whom he did not have any relationships. We had a very good discussion in his office about what needed to be done and the key need to build trust at the highest level of the customer organization. I set up European visits on agreed dates only for Heyer to cancel them. I visited him again and we set new dates. They were also cancelled. Despite continuing efforts on my part, the visits never took place. I later became aware that suffering cancellations of appointments was not something that only I experienced. A former executive at Turner Broadcasting Inc., Heyer's former employer, told me that he admired Steve as someone to have working for him, but that he would never have worked for Steve.

Heyer left August 31, for a job as CEO of Starwood Hotels

and Resorts. A true measure of the man is that one of the first things he did was to give Pepsi a five-year contract with Starwood, even though an internal Starwood review team recommended renewal of Coke's contract. Happily, the business is now back with Coca-Cola, demonstrating that this was pettiness on behalf of Steve. In many ways, it defined the man. His tenure at Starwood was short-lived.

I immediately began the search for a new chief corporate counsel. Deval Patrick had previously submitted his resignation to Daft. The *Boston Globe* reported that Patrick had resigned after Daft reneged on a promise to approve an independent investigation into allegations that Coca-Cola hired right-wing death squads to terrorize union organizers in Colombia.

Deval had a change of heart when I was named CEO, telling me he would consider staying, but I told him there was too much water under the bridge. He and another top executive were absolutely at war with each other. Deval clearly had other ambitions and had remained a resident of Boston, commuting every week to Atlanta. We were able to work out his departure amicably. He remained until the end of the year, which meant I had time to find a successor. I believe that once a person has made a decision to leave it's rare that a change of mind proves to be successful. Part of a psychological contract has been broken and when it is in the public domain, relationships are already redefined.

Only two years after leaving Coke, Deval was elected Governor of Massachusetts.

We began the search for a new corporate counsel, seriously interviewing Eric Holder, the current U.S. attorney general, until he withdrew from consideration. We eventually chose Geoffrey Kelly, an Australian and very able company insider. Meanwhile,

Daft had promised Sandy Allan, who was in charge of Europe, that he would also head North America, working out of his office in London and commuting to the U.S. That did not make sense to me nor to the Coke board and I nixed it, though Sandy was disgruntled after learning that he would not be in charge of nearly half the world. Sandy and I went all the way back to South Africa. He was the executive who refused to meet with me when he ran the independent National Beverages after Coke divested from South Africa. As group president, I had moved him to the Middle East, describing him to his face as "a bull in a china shop, but generally a good bull." He didn't like the description, but that is what he's like. Yet even though he broke a lot of china, I viewed him as a good executive for tough situations with his depth of company knowledge and strong work ethic.

I chose Cynthia McCague as Coke's new human resources director. Cynthia, who had been my HR director at CCHBC, was well-known and well-respected within the company and provided as smooth a transition in her new job as any executive could hope for given the momentous task I handed her.

Marketing, I have always believed, is the soul of the Coca-Cola Company. We had the world's most popular brand and yet with all the distractions of the previous few years, were losing our marketing edge. When I arrived, some of the television commercials were, in my opinion, atrocious. One particularly poor one featured a basketball player with a Coca-Cola stashed under his armpit; not a very appealing image. In the week before I became CEO, I attended the launch of C2, an ill-conceived midcalorie cola. It was strategically a weak proposition and the execution even weaker. Marketing of the new product was in the hands of people who had no "feel" for the brand. Within three weeks of becoming CEO, I named Chuck Fruit, who originally joined Coke from Anheuser Busch, as chief marketing officer to replace Dan Palumbo. Chuck righted the ship but sadly, ill health caused him to retire early. I also brought in Irial Finan, my successor at CCHBC, to head a newly formed Bottler Investment Group to oversee the company's wide range of ownership interests in bottlers worldwide, from Shanghai to Brazil. Some of these bottlers reported to group presidents, others to the Coca-Cola executive in charge of that country. Under the new structure, they would report to Irial and Irial would report directly to me. A body of opinion within the company was that we should divest of all our bottling interests. Implicit in that belief was that the Coca-Cola Company lacked the skills to competently run nuts-and-bolts, low-margin bottling companies. I, of course, had been running bottlers on and off for my entire career. Also, I believed divesting would reinforce the bottler's view that the company did not understand their business or care about it. The bottlers wanted leadership from the Coca-Cola Company, but as I reasserted it clashes arose over rights.

Here, too, there was a fundamental difference between my view and former management. The belief had been that by running the company with strict divisions of roles, neither "interfering" with the other, the relationship would be enhanced. In the short term, this was true. As a bottler, I had strived to have maximum independence. However, the truth was that we were one business, joined as I would put it, by veins and arteries, and that this is how the customers and consumers saw us. Remaining in our seemingly separate silos reduced disputes, but those disputes are at the heart of the benefits of the franchise structure, with the bottler's day-to-day skills meshing with the more long-term, strategic view which was the role of the franchisor. That we had recently taken a short-term view did not mean that we needed to fundamentally change the relationship, but primarily the way we at the Coca-Cola Company worked. We all knew this level of reengagement would be fractious, but was necessary for a functioning system and to avoid what had been happening: a hardening of the arteries.

That same summer, I made one of the most important decisions of my tenure, one that will continue to impact the company for years to come. Muhtar Kent, who had been so valuable to me in Eastern Europe, had gone on to head the European Division of Coca-Cola Amatil, the large Australian-based bottler. His promising career was derailed after authorities in Australia investigated Muhtar for insider trading of Amatil stock. Muhtar's financial advisor in late 1996 executed a short sale of 100,000 shares of Amatil stock just before the company issued an earnings warning. I believe it was an honest mistake. Muhtar's financial advisor had authority to execute stock trades on his behalf and made the short sale—essentially betting that the stock would soon go down—without Muhtar's knowledge. Muhtar settled the controversy by paying $30,000 and relinquishing the $324,000 profit from the short sale. The real penalty was much greater. He was forced to leave his high-profile position at Amatil, which likely would have led him eventually to an executive's job at Coke headquarters. In 1998, Muhtar became CEO of Efes Beverage Group, a brewer and the largest shareholder of the Coca-Cola bottler in Turkey.

Muhtar and I had always stayed in touch and he had been

one of those who lobbied hard behind the scenes for me to become Chairman and CEO after Daft resigned. Shortly after the board offered me the job, John Hunter, whom I trusted completely, flew to Barbados to brief me on the state of the company. I commented on the fact that there was no clear insider candidate to be president and John agreed. A move I needed to take, I told John, was to appoint an international president and yet there, again, was another void. I could not envision anyone in the company who was competent to take that job either. "You should bring Muhtar back," John said. I had been thinking about Muhtar all along but John's recommendation sealed the deal. It was clear to many of us that Muhtar was one of the most talented executives in the Coca-Cola system. We had worked closely together during that intense period after the Wall fell in 1989 when there was no margin for error, yet at the same time success demanded rapid risk-taking. It was the ultimate proving ground. I knew what Muhtar could do.

He also has the rare talent of diplomacy that is invaluable in high-level international business. Muhtar's father, Necdet Kent, was a Turkish diplomat stationed in France during World War II who had saved Turkish Jews from the Holocaust. Necdet demanded that Nazis release eighty Jews who were on cattle cars on their way to German concentration camps, and when the Nazis refused he boarded one of the cars and would not leave until the Jews were freed.

Muhtar operated comfortably in the highest government circles, becoming not only a respected business leader but a confidant to national leaders such as Sali Ram Berisha, president of Albania. Muhtar also had the invaluable experience of having worked on both the franchisor and franchisee side of the company. He understood both sides of the business and had empathy for both.

I knew I was going to bring Muhtar back, the only question was when. Yet when I called him, he declined my offer. "After all this, how can I come back?" he said. A few weeks later, Muhtar reconsidered, telling me he would consider returning as a group president, but I did not make an immediate move. This was a controversial decision and I would have to wait until the timing was right.

My first overseas trips as CEO were to India and China, a signal of the future. I arrived in India to a media circus. Dozens of reporters wanted to interview me, yet I had vowed not to do any interviews until I had been on the job for one hundred days and fully understood the landscape. With more than thirty reporters staking out the hotel lobby, I had to enter and exit the hotel through a service elevator, walking through the kitchen to the rear door. You know you have arrived when you get to use the service elevator and leave the hotel with the garbage trucks. The Indian public relations staff wanted to tell the press that I had already left India, but I insisted, firmly, that we were not going to mislead the media.

Mary Minnick, who was in charge of Asia out of Hong Kong, was then the group president responsible for India. She had brought in a man named Patrick Siewert from Kodak to oversee China and India. The company had hired him with the thought that he had the potential to one day be a group president. Although very personable and persuasive, Siewert was really very lightweight in terms of any knowledge of the soft drink business. He tended to operate at the high social end of the managerial scale rather than get his hands dirty, which did not endear him to me. That's just not the way I operate.

At the time, Sanjay Gupta was in charge of India's operations. During a cocktail party with Coke's Indian Advisory Board, which included some of the country's leading business leaders, I was sidelined by at least three board members who told me Sanjay was just not up to snuff. The next day, Gupta had a presentation for me in the ballroom of a hotel, with booths displaying everything they were doing in India. I was shocked at the high cost of this presentation, which was exclusively for me. I also couldn't help but notice that each time we stopped at a booth and someone started presenting, Sanjay would interrupt and take over the presentation. I am a great one for watching body language. Almost without exception, you could see the fear the employees had for Sanjay. That night, Sanjay hosted a dinner for me at his house in Delhi which was on three beautiful acres, with 150 guests. There were traditional dancers, the best wines. It cost an absolute fortune and the company was picking up the tab. I later told Mary and Patrick I didn't think he was the right guy for the job. They strongly disagreed, saying he was a future group president. With all the other tasks before me at the time, I delayed replacing Sanjay immediately. There are limits to power. All I really had was an overall gut feeling and a few observations. That is not the way to overrule senior management.

Then it was on to Shanghai, to a company-owned bottler that was losing money. The plant manager was an old-timer I had known in Nairobi. He was good at keeping the old Shanghai bottling plant running but knew very little about marketing. I went out in the marketplace with him and it was patently obvious that he was not in control of his business. He, too, would later be replaced.

Next up were tense meetings with bottlers in Mexico City and Rio de Janeiro. Both groups of bottlers were unhappy. One of their core issues was that we were not investing enough money in the brands and were taking out large shares of the profit. The bottlers did not like the quality of our marketing and advertising. They believed we were not keeping our end of the bargain. We charged bottlers a premium price for concentrate but in exchange, we did the marketing and we were supposed to give bottlers superb advertising. Coca-Cola Company does the pull and the bottler does the push. When we don't do the pull right, the bottler yells, either because the quality of the advertising is not good enough or we are not spending enough. I had Chuck Fruit working in Atlanta to track how much we had been spending on marketing and advertising in relation to our volume and to inflation. Media prices had been increasing over the years much faster than general inflation and Chuck discovered that our spending had not been keeping pace. This was a major source of the friction with the bottlers. It was affecting their ability to compete and needed to be fixed.

My first board meeting was July 19–20. "You've elected me to do two things," I told the board members. "You have brought me here as Chairman and CEO to run the company, reporting to the board of directors. I will undertake that with due respect to the board. I will try to keep the board informed to the best of my ability in regard to strategy and my actions. But you've also elected me chairman of the board, which means you've asked me to lead the board. It is my intention, to lead." I know I did not always measure up to that high standard, but that was my intent.

In August, I met with another group of bottlers, this time in Spain, and this time they were happy, a welcome respite. Ivester as international president had attempted to do a bottler consolidation but had pulled back when they phoned Goizueta, very similar to the situation I had faced in Germany. Spain, like Germany, was a very good and strong system but the reality was it had stopped growing in the 1990s because their costs and prices were too high and there wasn't enough investment in the marketplace. As group president, I met with the Spanish bottlers, trying to rebuild the relationship. The younger bottlers, tough and on the brink of hostility, started that meeting with a list of complaints, including transshipments into Spain from Coca-Cola bottlers in Germany, which was allowed under European Union law. I told them there was no way I was going to break EU law. We then discussed consolidation. I tried to explain that it was all about effectiveness and efficiency. If they did not want to relinquish their individual bottling franchises, I suggested that they create a so-called "virtual anchor bottler" to lower costs through joint purchasing and a centralized computer system. They already had a central organization for selling with supermarket chains and other large customers so they understood the concept and saw how it could increase efficiency and lower costs.

"If you do that and take the costs out, then the power of the local ownership is still there," I told them. "That would be my preferred strategy." I was also tough, telling them I had never met a more disenchanted group of bottlers and if that was how they felt about the system, they should consider selling.

The elders then suddenly moved in and took over the discussion, replacing the young execs in a kind of good-cop, bad-cop routine. We had a very good dialogue over the weeks and months ahead, working together with local management.

When I became Chairman and CEO, Spain had become an absolute gem in the Coke system in Europe, obviously aided by the growth in the Spanish economy and was led by a very innovative marketeer, Marcos de Quinto. I think some of my best relationships and best friendships were with the Spanish bottlers. They were a true example of how the franchise system could and should work. I was thrilled when they won the Woodruff Award for the best division in the world in 2007 after having been consistently in the top three for a number of years.

At the 2004 Summer Olympics in Athens, I approached the chairman of Coke's Turkish bottler, which was partly owned by Efes Beverage Group, the company Muhtar now ran. "I just want to tell you that I'm going to come knocking on your door," I told the bottler. "I really need Muhtar back." He was devastated. "You have hurt me to my heart," he said. It would still be a number of months before I moved on this but I was laying the groundwork. Luckily, the Turkish system has continued to flourish under the leadership of Michael O'Neill.

Also that August, Claus Halle passed away in Atlanta. He was the former president of international, a man with immense and deep knowledge of the business. He also had the skills of an international diplomat, something I aspired to develop and which I value in Muhtar. Claus could mix at the highest levels. He also displayed an enormous attention to detail. In Atlanta, Claus built an exact replica of the hunting lodge his family had lost in East Germany after World War II. He had the original plans and he had it rebuilt, bringing in old-style artisans to do the work, which he personally supervised. Typical of the man, he had mapped out his funeral, exactly who would speak and the hymns. I was honored to be on the list of those he wanted to deliver eulogies. It was a very emotional funeral and I had to choke back the tears. He was a giant of Coca-Cola and a great mentor. His life story deserves a book of its own, including the time he swam the Elbe River to escape the advancing Russians at the end of World War II and his beginning at Coca-Cola as a truck driver.

The fall of 2004 brought great promise on the product development side of the company, the first really good news in a long while. We had developed a new diet cola, or we thought we had. It is more truthful to say we had a great name for a diet cola: Coke Zero. The name tested very well with consumers. It portrayed a stronger message than Diet Coke, which signaled fewer calories but not *zero* calories. So we had this great moniker. What would we do with it?

The first test version of Coke Zero included Splenda, the artificial sweetener that had just been approved for soft drinks. However, the research showed that only Splenda-loyal consumers liked it and that the new soft drink could be only moderately successful. In my opinion, Splenda had a distinct aftertaste, and I was opposed to using it for a new product with a great name like Coke Zero. At a meeting in September, I instructed the flavor scientists to use the original Coke formula for Coke Zero, which would be sweetened not with Splenda but with the best artificial sweeteners available from country to country.

A veteran flavor scientist quickly objected. "You can't do that," he said. "Mr. Goizueta and Mr. Woodruff before him instructed that we could never use the Coca-Cola formula in anything but Coca-Cola Classic."

My reply was simple, "When do you want a new letter?" You could have heard a feather drop.

Coke Zero, designed to taste as close as possible to Coke Classic, was the most successful product launch since Diet Coke, attracting lapsed users of Coca-Cola who didn't like the taste of Diet Coke and those who were cutting back on the number of Coke Classics they consumed. Now, they would be able to have one Coke Classic per day and two Coke Zeros. Coke Zero in 2009 became the thirteenth Coca-Cola brand to achieve more than $1 billion in annual retail sales. Just as important, Diet Coke continued to be strong and there was little "cannibalization."

One very high-profile customer gave Coke Zero an early try. I chaired a fundraising campaign for the Kennedy Center and attended an awards ceremony at the White House. At a cocktail party afterward, we were ushered in to be photographed with President George W. Bush and First Lady Laura Bush in front of the Christmas tree.

"This is thirsty work, Mr. President," I said. "You need a Diet Coke."

"You know that's what I drink," he replied.

"How you tried Coke Zero?" I asked.

He had not heard of it but we arranged for Coke Zero to be delivered to the White House. I received a handwritten thank-you note from the president saying that he had tried Coke Zero and he had not yet made up his mind as to whether he liked it better than his mainstay, Diet Coke. I have the letter framed at my house in Barbados.

The fourteenth billion-dollar brand, Minute Maid Pulpy,

was launched during my tenure as well, but I had far less input on this one, really only one word. "Wow," I said when a Chinese flavor scientist asked me to taste it. I knew it would be huge! Minute Maid Pulpy became the first billion-dollar Coke brand developed and launched in an emerging market. In April 2011, Del Valle, which Coke acquired in 2007 in a joint venture with our Latin American partner, Coca-Cola FEMSA, became the company's fifteenth billion-dollar brand, followed by Vitamin Water, also acquired on my watch. Coke Zero, Minute Maid Pulpy, Del Valle, and Vitamin Water, which were all launched or acquired on my watch, have provided a big boost to our bottom line, which we sorely needed, but it took time.

Meanwhile, the bottom line remained a serious problem. Reluctantly, we issued a statement on September 15, 2004, warning that profits would fall below analyst's expectations for the remainder of the year, sending the stock briefly below $40 per share. "The solutions are complex, requiring implementation over the next several years and making short-term benefits unlikely," we wrote in a statement. My strategy all along had been "go slow to go fast later." That is not what Wall Street wanted to hear, but it was the only way we were going to pull the company out of its deep malaise.

Two months later, I announced that we would spend an additional $400 million per year on advertising and made a plea for patience as we tried to right the company. The board backed me solidly, bolstered by Warren Buffett's unequivocal statement: "I bought into this company because I believed in the brand Coca-Cola. If this is good for Coca-Cola, then I'm fine with it." Wall Street, not surprisingly, was not impressed. It failed to see an immediate gain, only $400 million less per year in profits. Many analysts believed we were simply incapable of regenerating growth. The stock hovered barely above $40 and at one point dipped to $38.50. We couldn't allow the stock price to drive our long-term strategy but at the same time, we had to keep a close eye on it. There were legitimate concerns that if it dropped too low, the company could be a takeover target. At a function in New York, I ran into David Rubenstein, cofounder of the Carlyle Group, one of the world's largest private equity firms. He was talking about the possibility of having the first $50 billion leveraged buyout, in which investors buy a company, usually by taking on significant debt. "What's your market cap right now?" Rubenstein asked me. At that time it was about $96 billion. "Well, that's a bit out of our reach, for now," said Rubenstein. In addition to a possible threat of an LBO, it was long known that Nestle coveted Coke and would, if the price was right, consider a takeover. We had to grow revenue and improve the bottom line to move our stock price up again, or we risked losing control of the company.

The analysts and the press were not being kind and as the Pepsi stock price (not market cap) passed the Coca-Cola price, *The Wall Street Journal* carried a cartoon of me being kicked by a Pepsi can. I had been asked and agreed to return the company to health for the long term and that is what I intended to do. There were calls for further cost-cutting and while I preached eliminating waste, "chasing pennies down the hallway," I was not willing to take the knife to costs largely made up of salaries and wages when the morale of the employees was still so fragile. Clearly, these were not comfortable times for me. I was determined not to fail and to maintain our long-term focus, and the board, crucially, held with me.

Behind the scenes, outside of Wall Street's skeptical gaze, we began to redefine the Coca-Cola Company. It started on a rainy night in London in August 2004, when I gathered all my direct reports at a hotel, many of them arriving late because the streets of London were literally flooded.

We were going to develop a total growth plan for the company, not just new strategies and a mission statement. It would be a clearly defined path to growth, underpinned by a strong emphasis on our culture and drawing from our heritage, but also relevant to the future. It would be a road map for how to get the company growing again and sustain that growth over the long term. It would not be dictated from on high but developed organically by the company's top leaders, who had been disheartened by layoffs, lawsuits, a game of musical chairs in the CEO's office, and a lingering slump in profits. As I traveled the world, I detected a pent-up annoyance and anger. We needed to get everyone in and get it all out on the table, and then decide what we were going to do about it. We had been through a similar process at CCHBC and it had been very helpful. I asked CCHBC veterans Cynthia McCague and Irial Finan to help as we repeated that process on a much larger scale for Coca-Cola. The mission statement would be called the Manifesto for Growth. I consider it my single most important accomplishment as Chairman and CEO.

We already knew from an internal survey that many of our employees did not trust upper management. They just didn't believe we had a strategy or that we could grow. It was also clear that many of the executives had lost faith in our strongest asset, the Coca-Cola brand. In fact, when the chief financial officer, Gary Fayard, and I revealed our lower growth targets, a number of executives thought they were still too high. I remember saying that if we could not even reach the lowered goals, "We should all pack up and go home."

We gathered 150 of the company's top executives for a three-day meeting to kick off the project. As they walked into the hotel ballroom the walls were adorned with posters of cartoon characters that contained the verbatim quotes from the internal employee engagement surveys, which showed the level of discontent at Coke to be far higher than at our peer companies. "We don't trust management," read one quote from the survey. "Our marketing is terrible," read another. "We have no strategy," said another.

I went on stage to explain that we were going to spend the rest of the day in small groups of a dozen in order to validate, or not, the research. Essentially, this was the catharsis phase. The next day I opened by saying that the intellectual capacity to change the business was in this room and that together we would redesign the company over the next four months. During one of the first meetings, one executive suggested that the solution to Coke's financial problems was to purchase another big company just as Pepsi had done many years earlier when it purchased the snack food company, Frito-Lay.

"Why would we buy another company when we can't seem to figure out how to run this one?" I asked, rhetorically. "Or," I continued, "do we need to buy another company in order to run our company because we can't?" There was silence. This was a necessary intervention on my part and the only occasion when I came down hard.

As the meetings progressed, and the executives began to realize that they really were able to shape the future of the company, the enthusiasm grew exponentially. It was the realization of the Manifesto for Growth.

The manifesto was a road map for the company, spelling out, for example, that we would no longer venture outside our core business. We would not, for example, buy another movie studio or a snack food company. Yet it also redefined the company as something much more than an emotionless, profit-producing machine. It built on the power of Brand Coca-Cola and the belief that we could once again become an iconic company.

The manifesto has five basic principles:

- **People:** Be a great place to work where people are inspired to be the best they can be.
- **Portfolio:** Bring to the world a portfolio of quality beverage brands that anticipate and satisfy people's desires and needs.
- **Partners:** Nurture a winning network of customers and suppliers, creating mutual, enduring value.
- **Planet:** Be a responsible citizen that makes a difference by helping build and support sustainable communities.
- **Profit:** Maximize long-term return to shareowners while being mindful of our overall responsibilities.

In very simple language, the manifesto provided an honest assessment of where we were as a company and where we needed to go.

"There's something very special about the Coca-Cola Company," the manifesto began. "There's a sense of pride that comes from building brands people love and making the most of ourselves as a company and as individuals. That's the magic we need more of today."

The manifesto discussed "hard truths" about the Coca-Cola Company.

"In recent years, we've lacked a clear direction and a common understanding of our purpose as a company," the manifesto stated. "We've dealt with challenges reactively and separately, not as a team. We've been too focused on the short term."

The document also listed "some honorable truths," including the deep-seated belief that Coca-Cola could be a great company once again: "We believe a greater company lies within us. There's not a moment to lose as we rebuild our company."

Wall Street couldn't have cared less about the manifesto, which tends to look far beyond the next quarter's earnings statements. Yet the manifesto absolutely turned the company around in a way that was invisible from the outside. We rolled it out around the world. The top 150 executives were the authors. Yet it was implemented by the employees who, in general, were enthusiastic, even in the U.S., which tended to be jaded about such things. Board member Cathy Black, who had a background in publishing as CEO of Hearst Business Media Corp., was impressed, particularly with the simple language of the manifesto. "You had the courage to do this," she said. "I love it."

The manifesto provided Coca-Cola with a framework for who we are, a clarity of vision, and a clarity of tactics that soon started to permeate the company. Morale increased significantly among the very people we relied upon to produce the profit results Wall Street so desperately sought. It was similar, on a much larger scale, to the results we witnessed during those heady days in the Philippines as we rallied the employees at weekend meetings. I can't emphasize this enough: A company can't succeed unless it has its employees behind it. They have to be convinced that the leadership truly has their best interests at heart and can win for them. Now, we had that at Coca-Cola. It seems like an oversimplification to say this and perhaps it is, but the manifesto cemented the turnaround at Coca-Cola. For the first time, our allies were the employees we needed most to achieve our goals. It became *their* plan; they owned it and believed in it. No edict from the mount or sales job was needed.

The new program broke the back of negativity and I now had the company in my hands. The employees trusted me and believed in me. Yet this was not about me. It was a long-term strategy. I had agreed to stay no more than five years and by the time we rolled out the manifesto, almost a year had elapsed. I wanted to put in place a strategy that had legs and life and would shape the company—long after I was relaxing again in Barbados—a truly sustainable strategy my successor would embrace and build upon. When asked what my legacy would be, I always replied that I would not have one unless my successor was successful.

Coca-Cola had relied too heavily on the success of the past, recalled Tom Mattia, who was my vice president and director of public affairs and communications. With the manifesto, we began looking toward the future.

The manifesto was realized in many tangible ways, including the expansion of company programs to solve environmental problems. The main focus was on water, which is so vital to the production of Coca-Cola and over which we had been heavily criticized, particularly in India. Water tables there dropped as a result of drought and overuse in agriculture, yet Coke was blamed. In fact, after we closed one plant in India, the water table continued to recede at the same rate. Nevertheless, when water supplies dwindled, Coca-Cola, with its high international profile, was always a magnet for criticism. Water shortages were not good for the company's image or for the communities we served. It was in the best interest of both Coca-Cola and our customers for the company to employ its resources to preserve the water supply, even if we were not the cause of it being diminished. In 2005, we partnered with the U.S. Agency for International Development and our bottlers to reduce water usage in our plants, preserve watersheds, and build water treatment stations for local villages.

"No company is doing more than Coke to provide clean water to the world's poor (and not-so-poor) people," *Fortune* magazine wrote of our efforts, which are still ongoing and growing.

Tom Mattia remembers that the manifesto influenced the decision of where to place a bottling plant in Pakistan. The original site, close to Karachi, was in a water-stressed community. With "planet" a key part of our mission statement, we moved the plant farther from Karachi to an area with more water.

That was both a business decision and an environmental one, and yet they really are one and the same. Coke's business could only succeed if the community where we sold our products also thrived. Clearly, a community without an adequate water supply is not going to thrive. The manifesto recognized that the factors were all related and should be incorporated in the company's day-to-day business decisions. "It was still a pure business decision," Tom said of the Pakistan bottling plant location. "But it was a pure business decision viewed a different way. The manifesto did give us a very different view of the world."

As we went about constructing the manifesto, we still had lingering clouds over our heads. One of the most troubling was the U.S. Securities and Exchange Commission investigation into a practice known as "channel stuffing" in Japan from 1997–1999. It's fair to say that this controversy was a direct result of the malaise that hit the company after Roberto's death and the sloppy attempts to fix it through mass layoffs, which created fear and dissension throughout the ranks. When that happens, all sorts of other things go wrong.

An employee wrote a letter to then president Steve Heyer and Deval Patrick, the general counsel, detailing allegations of wrongdoing including channel stuffing, also called "gallon pushing"—artificially pumping up concentrate sales to bottlers to boost corporate earnings in a given quarter. The complaining employee was scheduled to be fired in the latest round of layoffs.

Heyer apparently ignored the letter. Deval may have read it but did not intercede to prevent the employee from being fired as scheduled. Firing a whistle-blower is never a good idea since it can legally be construed as retaliation for making the complaint. Gary Fayard, then the company's chief financial officer, tried to stop the firing, but it was too late. "We fired him this morning," Gary was told when he called the employee's division.

The controversy was now forced into the public arena. Not surprising, the newly unemployed employee filed a lawsuit against Coke. His allegations also sparked a federal investigation. Coke had, it turned out, rigged Burger King's marketing test of frozen Coke by hiring teenagers to buy them. Coke apologized to Burger King and paid $21 million in damages.

In the meantime, the company, and Gary specifically, had to deal with the lengthy SEC investigation on channel stuffing.

Gary and the company's top lawyer, Deval Patrick, clashed on this issue.

Deval left the company shortly after I became CEO when I refused to rescind his resignation, primarily because of the severe friction between Deval and another executive (not Gary). The SEC investigation reached a critical point in December 2004, about six months after I returned to the company.

As the case progressed, Gary's lawyer told him it was increasingly likely that the SEC would proceed with a civil action against him. Gary's lawyer told him he was 99 percent confident they could fight the case and win, but it could take five years to litigate and this could ruin his career. Gary discussed the matter with his wife Nancy, who thought that he should defend his reputation and fight any civil action brought against him by the SEC.

Gary came to see me and offered to resign. "My lawyer is telling me that the odds of a civil action are fairly high and, based on that, I can no longer function as CFO," he told me. "I will have to leave. That is the only thing I can do."

I refused to accept the resignation. "Gary, you're innocent and we are going to fight this with you," I told him.

Over Christmas, Gary got a call from Herbert Allen, a Coke board member. "I just wanted to call and wish you Merry Christmas and to tell you the board will stand by you," Herbert said. Don Keough, then retired and serving on the Coke board, also called with a similar message of support. This reflects the caliber of the Coke board I served: men and women of great principle.

Ultimately, the SEC investigation was resolved in April 2005. All of the company's accounting disclosures were accurate. Nevertheless, the SEC found that the company failed to disclose the impact of channel stuffing on future earnings, and made false and misleading statements in a public filing. In the settlement, Coke neither admitted nor denied the SEC findings and the company paid no fine, but we did agree to strengthen our internal disclosure review process. Gary was not sanctioned and remains the Coca-Cola CFO to this day.

There was now one less cloud hanging over the company. Yet others still lingered. In 1999 a group of African American employees sued the company, claiming discrimination in pay and promotions. The company settled the case a year later and agreed to allow an independent task force to monitor our hiring practices. The task force, chaired by former U.S. Labor Secretary Alexis Herman, was scheduled to be dismantled in 2005, but I personally appeared before U.S. District Judge Richard Story and asked him to extend it another year. We were in compliance with the settlement but still lacked adequate commitment to the larger goal of diversity, I told the judge. He replied that he had never heard of anyone asking for an extension of court supervision. Many people thought I had taken leave of my senses. However, I believed diversity was not only the correct moral goal; it was good for business and would make Coca-Cola a stronger company.

"Our company and our leadership must be as inclusive as our brands . . . as diverse talent proliferates, ideas and innovation thrive as well," I wrote at the time.

We concluded the case a year later on an extremely positive note. Judge Story praised our efforts and invited us to go to dinner with him at his favorite barbecue joint in Atlanta together with the plaintiffs, their lawyers, and members of the task force.

In another sign of the goodwill generated from that case, Alexis Herman, head of the task force for six years, joined the Coca-Cola board of directors in 2007 and is still there today.

Yet another legal controversy ended in late 2004 when we settled the European Commission's antitrust suit. As a result of our strong and hard-earned market position, the commission was concerned we were stifling competition. In Belgium, for example, we had a 68 percent market share compared to 5 percent for Pepsi. In France, it was 60 percent Coke, 6 percent Pepsi. In the settlement, we agreed to a long list of changes designed to foster competition. For example, we would allow retailers to devote up to 20 percent of the space in Coke bottler–owned coolers to competing products.

"Consumers will generally have more choice at cafés, pubs, and shops and will, therefore, be in a position to choose on the basis of price and personal preferences rather than pick up a Coca-Cola product because it's the only one on offer," the EU's Competition Commissioner, Mario Monti, said in a statement.

I met personally with Monti before we announced the settlement. He wanted assurances that we were sincere about fulfilling the agreement. Our meeting had been scheduled for thirty minutes but lasted twice that long. We discussed not only the settlement but also business philosophy. Monti and I warmed to each other. That meeting sealed the deal in terms of us having no fine and admitting no guilt but with administrative agreements for future conduct. We did indeed take the agreement seriously and I would later retire Sandy Allan for, in my opinion, violating the spirit of that agreement. I advised the Competition Commission accordingly.

After Monti left the Competition Commission, I asked him

to join Coca-Cola's international advisory board, another sign, I believe, of the goodwill we were building throughout the world. I don't think anyone could have imagined that the competition commissioner who had been pursuing Coca-Cola would later join the Coca-Cola family, but he did. The perception of the company was starting to change for the better throughout the world. As the lawsuits were resolved one by one, former adversaries were joining our ranks, a sign of the company's growing respect and integrity. The embattled atmosphere of the post-Goizueta era was dissipating.

There was more good news in October 2006, when a federal judge in Miami dismissed lawsuits against two Coca-Cola bottlers in Colombia for allegedly hiring right-wing paramilitaries to kill union leaders. The company had been dismissed from the lawsuit in 2003 and now the litigation—groundless from day one but a distraction and harmful to Coke's image—was effectively over.

As we worked through the checklist of legal problems that were, one by one, being resolved, I did manage to make time for family. Cara, who was then the volunteer director for the Atlanta Humane Society, convinced me one Christmas to dress as Santa Claus and to be photographed with dogs on my lap. Getting dogs to sit on your lap to have their photograph taken isn't easy, yet it was a welcome respite from the pressures at Coke as well as enjoyable for the family. Only one person recognized that Santa was the CEO of Coke.

At the same time, I received regular visits in my office by a nurse to check my blood pressure, which was elevated from the stress. This was not something I told Pamela because it was, of course, what she feared when I took the job.

With the legal distractions fading, it was time to increase my focus on the business of selling soft drinks. In China we launched an accelerated plan to boost growth because we were losing to Pepsi. China remains a tough battle although Minute Maid Pulpy has greatly boosted our efforts.

One region of the world that rarely gave me any trouble was Latin America under the brilliant leadership of Pacho Reyes, who remains a close friend, and the many great bottlers, including Coca-Cola FEMSA. Just before I retired, Pacho, Pamela, and I traveled to Machu Picchu, the fifteenth-century Inca ruin in Peru, to celebrate five great years together. Without the consistent growth of volume and profits in Latin America, the turnaround of Coca-Cola would have been much more difficult, if not impossible.

I brought Muhtar back to the company in May 2005 as head of North Asia, Eurasia, and the Middle East, including Japan and China, moving Mary Minnick to head of marketing to replace Chuck Fruit who did a great job but was having health problems and, sadly, died just after I retired. Mary was a brilliant marketeer but was not a strong general manager. She was not aggressive enough in Japan, India, or China, I believed. Initially, she balked at the marketing job, believing it would be a demotion. I had a solution I had been considering for a long time as a way to break down some of the walls that slowed and often impeded bringing new brands and new ideas to the market. I offered to give her technical and strategic planning in addition to marketing, bringing her back into the Atlanta headquarters in a very powerful position, although I also allowed her to maintain an office in London, which was a defensible move given the creative ideas which emanated from Europe. It also met Mary's personal needs and demonstrated the flexibility a company needs to retain top-class female executives. I chose Patrick Siewert, the former Kodak executive, to head the Southern Asia and Pacific Group including India and the Philippines, which proved to be a mistake. Patrick did not work out. I found him to be an inadequate manager. I did not listen to my own gut or some of the people around me, but relied on a professional evaluation system. That was a mistake.

Before hiring Muhtar, I contracted an outside law firm to compile a report on the insider trading controversy. It reinforced my belief that the incident was an honest mistake by Muhtar's financial advisor. The Coca-Cola board was also comfortable with the report and with my decision. These were some of the most respected business leaders in the world, including Warren Buffet and Peter Ueberroth. It was not a patsy board, as you will see later in this chapter. They backed Muhtar, despite a smattering of press criticism. I must say, however, that there were executives even within my inner circle who questioned my decision. We just chose to disagree.

My vision for Muhtar at the time was for him to eventually become international president and then we would see, based on his performance, whether he would be a candidate to succeed me. He had to earn it. Muhtar had no assumptions of eventually becoming CEO. He would frequently say, "I will leave when Neville leaves." He saw us as binary and in a way, we were. Mary Minnick was also seen as possible successor as were a few outside candidates we had identified.

Coca-Cola Enterprises, the company's largest bottler, which had franchises in North America and Europe, was a particularly troublesome challenge.

CCE was a perennial underperformer and its leaders held a long-standing grudge against the Coca-Cola Company, which had created the company in 1986 by merging company-owned bottlers in North America with two other independent bottlers, the John T. Lupton franchises and BCI Holding Corporation's plants. In 1991, CCE merged with Summerfield Johnson's family-owned company, the Chattanooga-based Johnston Coca-Cola Bottling Group, Inc., one of Coke's oldest bottlers. CCE later expanded into Europe as well.

Many in the CCE ranks believed Coke bested CCE in the negotiations, overcharging them for the company-owned bottling franchises and leaving CCE with a crippling debt. There had been, of course, a willing buyer and a willing seller and more important, these were perpetual franchises—not subject to periodic renewal by Coke and therefore legitimately priced at a premium. So it didn't make much sense to me for CCE to complain later about the transaction. Still, the resentment lingered and remained a strong factor in the often tense relationship between Coke and CCE.

There was some arrogance at CCE. In my early days with the company, the U.S. bottlers were the gold standard. They were the source of new ideas and it was to the U.S. where bottlers from other countries would travel to learn. By the time I became CEO in 2004, it had become embarrassing to bring visitors through the U.S. marketplace. The execution was very poor. Some of the private-label colas actually had better packaging than CCE. Yet executives at CCE believed they were still the best. In fact, bottlers in Brazil, France, Spain, South Africa, and other countries were the new gold standard.

I met privately with the CCE board chair, Lowry Kline, in

February 2005 and flatly told him that John Alm, the company CEO, did not have my confidence. Lowry then allowed me to meet with nonexecutive board members. It was a tough meeting, with the CCE board members still maintaining the view that many of their problems were due to overpayment to Coke for the bottlers. They had been convinced that most of their problems were caused by the Coca-Cola Company. At this point, I was able to tell them about the $400 million in new marketing money—$150 million of that dedicated to North America, which placated them somewhat. Then I raised the issue of management. I told them that while it was not my role to choose the management of a public company, I was entitled, as the franchisor, to a view about the quality of the management. I laid out a strong case as to why Alm should not be running the business. The board disagreed and word soon leaked to Alm about the meeting. It did not help the already strained relationship with CCE. One of the problems with huge bottling franchises like CCE is that while they make sense economically, they sometimes lose sight of the interdependencies of the system, particularly when they are publicly held companies like CCE. Yet by the end of 2005, Alm was out and a new CEO, John Brock, was in.

That did not, however, solve our problems with CCE. Brock launched a series of retail price increases, trying to boost the company's profit margins, but in doing so, eroded Coke market share, thus reducing our concentrate sales. We had no choice but to raise concentrate prices. It was a bitter, tit-for-tat exchange.

Hoping to find a solution for the deep-seated problems in North America, I presented to CCE's board in the spring of 2006 a plan called "Project Diesel." CCE in the U.S. would merge with the remaining independent bottlers in order to lower costs and increase profit. We had calculated that we could pay a real premium for the independent bottlers and easily recoup the investment by increasing the scale and efficiency of the bottling operations. The CCE board flatly rejected the idea, an outgrowth of the lack of trust they had for Coca-Cola. When the news leaked, the proposal caused a lot of dissatisfaction with the independent bottlers who thought we were favoring CCE and worried about the price they would receive in the acquisition. Don Knauss, who had been appointed head of Coca-Cola USA, had put an enormous amount of time into this effort and when Clorox offered him the job of Chairman and CEO, he moved on.

It was then time, I believed, to bite the bullet and make a full-fledged move to buy CCE. I went around to Coke board members, including Warren Buffet, to sell them on the plan. The logic was something the board members found difficult to disagree with. It made economic sense to buy CCE. The devil, however, was in the details.

This would be a takeover. CCE stock at the time was around $18.50 per share. We thought we could make a bid at $23. Yet our bid would be open-ended. Hedge funds and other investors could launch a bidding war, driving up the CCE stock price far beyond what we thought we should pay. In a normal acquisition, we could have just walked away if the bidding got out of hand. That was not an option in this case for two reasons: We would have completely lost credibility if we walked away, and in the eyes of CCE we would have appeared incredibly weak. Also, another bidder might have acquired the company, leaving us potentially with a far more difficult partner than CCE. The board recognized this and I backed down. In my view, I had failed. Yet I softened the ground for an acquisition and in 2010, after I retired, Coke did acquire the North American business of CCE. This time, CCE approached Coke. No longer was it a takeover, and this time the deal worked. I didn't do the deal, but I believe I started the process that led to the deal.

I also explored other possible acquisitions. The moral of the following story is that personal prejudice and business strategy sometimes get confused. It all started when we held a meeting of Coke's top management in Barbados. We played golf with Gary Player, a South African and one of the best golfers of all time who has long been a close friend of Coca-Cola. Over lunch and dinner, we noticed that Gary ate no meat or dairy products. He is a vegan and told us how it had stopped the progression of his arthritis. A few months later, Pamela decided to become a vegan and much to her surprise, I joined her. It caused a great flurry at Coca-Cola. Now I had to have vegan food everywhere I went around the world. I found the vegan diet to be very good for me. I lost weight and my cholesterol dropped. One key component of the vegan diet is soy milk and I began looking around for companies that had a strong market presence in soy products. We considered several of them and had informal discussions with Coke board members during a meeting at Pebble Beach, California, but they didn't like the deal. They thought the price was too high and were worried that it would distract us from our core business. Muhtar was also opposed to the acquisition, one example of honest disagreement between the two of us.

I'm not sure they would have voted against me, but I decided not to push the issue. In retrospect, the board was right.

The stock of one of the companies has subsequently plunged, reflecting a serious downturn in its profitability.

The Coca-Cola board was strongly supportive of me but did exercise strong and appropriate oversight. An analyst once asked me what I was going to do about my strong board. I replied, "I therefore assume you would want me to have a weak one." There was no reply. I worked well with almost all the board members, including Buffett, Ueberroth, former U.S. Senator Sam Nunn of Georgia, Herbert Allen, and Jim Robinson. Yet I had a chilled relationship with Bob Nardelli, CEO of Home Depot. In March 2005, the Compensation Committee was reviewing bonuses for 2006. Normally, the committee approved bonuses for the top fifty executives, and management decided the remainder. Bob had called me and asked for the full bonus list and I agreed. It included a list of one thousand bonuses, all within plan but also based on a level of discretion based on individual performance. Bob came to the meeting with the big bonus list well thumbed and marked with yellow highlighter. He then asked why two junior awards differed, to which I replied, "I have no idea. I delegate those kinds of decisions and they are according to plan." Two very different management styles had clashed. While I prefer my own model, both are effective in their own way and under certain circumstances, Bob's works best in the short term. Bob is very detail oriented, very bright, and extremely hard working but he and I were on different wavelengths and just never hit it off. Bob, to his credit, realized this and left the board in 2005. Another board member, J. Pedro Reinhard, former chief financial officer of Dow Chemical, ran afoul of that company's board for allegedly plotting a leveraged buyout of Dow without authorization from the board and without telling the CEO. I discovered that he never supported my strategy, although he never raised any issues directly during board meetings. When he left Dow, he had to formally resign from the Coke board since he no longer had the same position as when he was named a director. When a director changes jobs, the Coke board usually allows them to remain as a director. However, this time I persuaded the board not to renew Pedro's appointment.

As we pushed to regenerate sales and profit, I tried to instill in Coca-Cola the spirit of frugality that many bottlers, out of necessity, had long possessed. Coca-Cola, with its traditional high profit margins, had never been forced to "chase pennies down the hallway." We always did things Rolls-Royce style. One of the most disturbing examples was a $3 million party in Johannesburg, featuring the rapper Snoop Dogg, after South Africa was awarded an internal prize, the Woodruff Cup, for superior performance. I wanted to change that mindset, starting with my own office where the company had been scheduled to spend $1 million for renovations. I stopped that. We did recarpet but scrounged furniture from other offices instead of buying new. I also eliminated expensive wines in the corporate aircraft. These were small things, but small things that delivered messages.

In March 2005, Klaus Maurers, the German bottler with whom I had developed a close friendship, came to see me. We had a long, detailed discussion of how we could accomplish a one-bottler strategy. This time, we got it done. Finally, the consolidation of the German bottler system which I had begun in the mid-1980s was complete. Sometimes, change demands extreme patience.

Bottler consolidation has been a common story throughout

my career, but bringing it about in Japan has been extremely difficult.

Japan is a very important market for Coca-Cola. It is one of the most profitable in the world, primarily because of the sale of coffee in cans. The one million Coca-Cola vending machines are specially designed to dispense hot drinks in winter and cold in summer.

It's a really delicate trick to hold a really hot can between two fingers and sip it without burning your lips but the Japanese have mastered it.

There is a plethora of innovative brands in Japan; even the most successful are only successful for a year. It's an extremely competitive market and it takes a completely different mind-set to operate in Japan.

One of the most difficult bottler consolidation challenges involved the bottler in Tokyo owned by the Takanashi family. After years of negotiation, the family decided to sell a 34 percent stake to Coca-Cola in 2007 when I was CEO and Chairman. During final negotiations, which I attended, the family members asked to meet again the next day. That evening, they went to the grave of their father and "consulted" with him. The next morning, they signed the agreement.

Slowly, with all the key pieces of our strategy in place, we began to see strong and steady spikes in sales, profits, and dividends. The stock topped $65, further bolstering morale for employees who owned Coca-Cola stock and had stock options, which now would actually be worth something. The financial crisis of 2008 set us back, but only temporarily, and as I write this the stock price has rebounded.

As profitability increased, friction between the bottlers and

North Avenue began to fizzle. It's like a marriage. When a marriage is going badly, the partners fight over the tiniest of issues. You can find fault even with how your spouse parks the car. When a marriage is going well, you might find the spouse's car-parking technique quite amusing, and tease them lovingly about it.

Coca-Cola in the late 1990s had "lost its way" Muhtar recalled. The bottlers and Coke were fighting over a shrinking profit base, and a fading belief in the power of the brand. "We became arrogant," Muhtar continued. "We lost touch with the details of what makes this business work well. Neville and I were able to bring back the belief that Coca-Cola is great, and that we can grow again. When you believe that, when you have a growth model, no one quibbles over trying to split something that is shrinking."

There was time now, and money, to look beyond profit, to some of the "Ps" in the manifesto such as "planet" and "partnership."

In 2006, we agreed, along with other beverage companies, to halt sales of full-caloried beverages in U.S. public schools, an initiative launched by the American Heart Association and former president Bill Clinton.

First, an editorial comment. I believe it's unfair to single out the beverage industry for diabetes and obesity. When I think back on my childhood in Africa, and the five-mile bike rides each way to school and my lifelong participation in sports, I can't help but believe that computers, video games, television, and the lack of physical exercise might be more responsible than soft drinks for overweight schoolchildren.

That said, the beverage industry had pushed too far in the schools, actually putting soda machines not only in high schools but in middle schools as well. When children are in school, their parents have no control over what they are consuming. So in that respect, soda machines in schools might have interfered with a responsible parent's efforts to manage their child's diet.

So Coca-Cola and our competitors were open to Clinton's idea to address this issue as part of a voluntary program. Don Knauss, as head of Coca-Cola USA at the time and with whom I worked well, presented me with a draft of the agreement, but it didn't make sense to me. It called for the withdrawal of all soft drinks, even diet soda. Clearly, without sugar and calories, diet soda doesn't contribute to diabetes or obesity. At the same time, schools were going to allow sports drinks and juice drinks, both with a full-sugar content, to remain along with snack machines. Yet we would have to stop selling products with zero calories?

"The problem is aspartame," the artificial sweetener, I was told. I refused to buy that argument. "This is about calories," I said, adding that there was absolutely no evidence of any health risk from aspartame. Even though the rest of the industry had approved the agreement, I told Don, "I'm not going to sign off on it." Don agreed to revisit the issue.

Ten days later, I presented Clinton with the J. William Fulbright Prize for International Understanding, an award which Coca-Cola sponsors. After Clinton arrived and we were waiting in the greenroom before going on stage, I noticed the former president was drinking a Diet Coke, as was his habit.

"Mr. President, glad to see you are still drinking Diet Coke," I said.

"That's my drink," he replied.

"It's a terrible pity that kids are no longer going to be able to drink it in high schools."

Clinton was unaware that the agreement banned diet sodas. He agreed that this was illogical. "Leave it with me and I will sort it out," said Clinton.

Twenty-four hours later, diet sodas were back among the allowable offerings. There are times when as CEO, logic requires that you must stand your ground, but luck also helps as I was able to address Clinton at an informal moment.

Later that year, Coke agreed to donate land in downtown Atlanta valued at the time at $10 million for a new civil rights museum. Atlanta was the home of the late Martin Luther King Jr. and was the center of the civil rights movement. The land was the remaining piece of a large tract the Coca-Cola Company had assembled in the heady 1980s for a new office block. A large portion of the acreage had already been donated to Home Depot cofounder Bernie Marcus, for his project to build the world's largest and best aquarium. It was followed by an expanded "World of Coca-Cola" museum and both have been hugely successful. This made the remaining land very much sought after by other groups wanting to tie in with these attractions.

As head of the Atlanta Committee for Progress, I worked very closely with Atlanta mayor Shirley Franklin, who was a very effective leader. She was trying to regenerate the city after the failed tenure of Mayor Bill Campbell, who was later imprisoned for tax evasion. Shirley convinced me that our land would be the right location for a museum that would have a broader appeal than the Martin Luther King Center. When built, it will represent the role Atlanta played as "the city too busy to hate."

In Beijing in June 2007, we announced a $20 million donation to the World Wildlife Fund to help conserve seven of the world's most important freshwater river basins. The partnership with WWF continues to this day and I am a board member of this very vital and effective organization.

There was also now time to enjoy the job and enjoy life.

One of the most emotional moments of my life was attending a rugby match between England and Ireland in Dublin's Croke Park, site of the infamous "Bloody Sunday," which took place on November 21, 1920, during the struggle for Irish independence from Great Britain. On that day, British police opened fire inside the stadium, killing twelve innocent spectators during a rugby match, in retaliation for the Irish Republican Army's killing of fourteen British intelligence officers earlier that day. That night, three IRA prisoners being held at Dublin Castle were tortured and shot by their British captors.

Croke Park was hallowed ground. Further complicating matters was the fact that rugby was traditionally seen as an English sport, despite the fact that Ireland played international rugby as an integrated island with Northern Ireland—which is part of the United Kingdom—as if the division of 1922 had never taken place. Even so, for many years anyone who played Gaelic football would be banned from the game for life if caught inside a British rugby stadium. Such are the complexities of Ireland.

There was even opposition in 2007 to the England-Ireland match at Croke Park. On the third attempt, the Gaelic Football Association approved temporary use while the rugby stadium a few miles away was being redeveloped. History leaves a heavy footprint.

Security was very tight as Irish and English teams played at the park on February 24, 2007. No one knew how the crowd would react when the English anthem was played. There was absolute dead silence in the stadium, not a single note of dissension among the eighty thousand fans. It was a moment of true reconciliation, a truly historic moment. I looked around the Coca-Cola box and almost to a person, everyone was crying. Grown men and former rugby players do cry! At that moment, I felt history being thrown over my shoulder.

Six weeks later, the president of Ireland, Mary McAleese, was in Atlanta and I had breakfast with her and her husband. We discussed the emotional power of that day at Croke.

"Did you see me as I was leaving the field when I paused before walking up the steps?" she asked. "The reason I paused wasn't theatrical. My legs were collapsing under me. I didn't think I could walk up the steps. I was so emotional." Rugby had helped to change the mindset just as it had in South Africa when Nelson Mandela employed it to help unite the country after the fall of apartheid.

As CEO, I made several nostalgic trips back to South Africa. As we flew down on the company plane, I told my executive assistant, John Brownlee, a young African American lawyer, that he would find that blacks and whites in South Africa are more integrated than they are in the United States. He did not believe me.

"Whatever, boss," Brownlee recalls thinking at the time. We even made a small bet. Yet when we boarded the plane to return to Atlanta, John conceded that I was correct in this perception. After touring South Africa for the first time, he could see the true racial transformation of the post-apartheid era and more genuine social interaction between the races than he was used to. He conceded the bet. Race continues, however, to cast a shadow over South Africa.

Pamela and I attended the 2007 Academy Awards Ceremony, the year Helen Mirren won best actress for her role in *The Queen*. During a party after the ceremonies, a photographer's scout mistook Pamela for Mirren and began leading her away to do a television interview. When I discovered the mistake, I led the scout to the real Helen Mirren, whom I had spotted a few minutes earlier. She and Pamela were wearing similar dresses. Mirren laughed when I told her of the mistake. "Can I hold your Oscar?" I asked Mirren. She handed it to me and I kissed her. This was one of the perks of the job and after all, "All work and no play make Jack a dull boy."

The 2008 Olympics in Beijing were extremely successful for both Coca-Cola and China. Three years earlier, I stood on the Great Wall of China as Coca-Cola extended its Olympic sponsorship for another twenty years. The sponsorship stretches back, uninterrupted, to 1928.

The Beijing Olympics, however, were not without controversy. I had to address concerns from the actress Mia Farrow and others who accused China of "bankrolling Darfur's genocide," and demanded Coke cancel sponsorship of the games. While Farrow was raising money to fight Coca-Cola, not one penny of it was to aid Darfur. I challenged her on this in the media but never received a reply.

China's critics fail to realize that progress is of necessity an evolutionary process. How long did it take for blacks and women to obtain the right to vote in the U.S.? It took generations, a sad commentary on history. It's unrealistic to expect China's transformation to occur overnight, as well. Isolating China won't hasten that transformation.

During the Beijing Olympics, as Pamela and I would leave

events, we would shake the hands of Chinese spectators, looking directly into their eyes and saying, "Thank you." The smiles they generated spoke a thousand words. We became quite close to our volunteer driver and guide, a university professor. She spent a week with us and even brought her daughter to meet us. She described it as the most wonderful week of her life and insisted on giving us a farewell gift as we were leaving. Those are the one-on-one encounters that happened at the Olympics that Mia Farrow never understood. Think of the small childhood impressions we all have. I still remember the Nigerian police officer who stayed with us in Ireland when I was a child and the time I witnessed men flogged with whips in Angola. That created in my young mind a point of view, an enlightened, different point of view. When our driver's daughter met us, she perhaps gained a different perception of Westerners. Through individual contact you break the propaganda machine. Journalists may write that China has made little progress in human rights. It's simply not true, although clearly, the progress is not sufficient. The change may not be perceptible from our perspective but it is real and will quicken over time.

My time as Chairman and CEO began to quickly come to an end. I had promised Pamela that I would stay in the job five years, yet my plan was to serve the last year as chairman only, turning over the job of CEO to my successor. In early 2007, I named Muhtar, who had performed superbly since his return to the company, as president of Coca-Cola. It was clear then that Muhtar would be my successor, although he still had to complete extensive interviews for the job with me and members of the board of directors. Mary Minnick decided to leave the company but did so with elegance on her part and we still remain in contact.

Succession planning is a crucial but often difficult challenge for large corporations. One of the tragedies of corporate life is that you see a number of embittered former CEOs. Sometimes it's because they have failed in their positions. More often than not, however, it's because they have stayed on far too long. In their latter years, they devote much of their energy toward preserving their jobs. They don't work on succession because succession is a threat. Another problem is that those executives who are capable of becoming successful CEOs won't sit around indefinitely as second in command. They'll leave to run their own companies somewhere else if their boss lingers too long. There are exceptions of course, such as Don Keough, who was a powerful and effective leader as second in command at Coca-Cola and was even viewed by many as a co-CEO. In many companies, however, the long-serving second in command is more of an acolyte than a leader and is not really qualified to take over when the boss finally does step down, thus creating a poor succession. As Coca-Cola learned all too painfully, that can set a company back for years.

Since I had established a five-year limit from day one, I would not fall into that trap of hanging on too long. It did mean, however, that I had to start looking for a successor almost immediately. I was fortunate to have Muhtar. He was part of the team that helped me build the long-term strategy, guaranteeing continuity for the company when I retired. He could take the strategy and build it to the next level.

I retired for the second time in the spring of 2009, returning to the life we had planned, alternating between Barbados, France, and Atlanta. Cara and her husband Zak Lee, a Georgia native whom she met at the University of South Carolina, moved to Barbados as well. They have blessed Pamela and me with a delightful grandson, Rory. Zak was the international marketing manager for a golf community in Barbados called Moonshine Ridge.

Coca-Cola has thrived under Muhtar's leadership, with consistently higher earnings and dividend increases. In 2011 the company ranked sixth on *Fortune*'s list of the world's fifty most admired companies. Pepsi ranked twenty-sixth. In the U.S., Diet Coke surpassed Pepsi to become the second most poplar soft drink, trailing only Coca-Cola. As I handed over the reins of the Coca-Cola Company to Muhtar, I was often asked, "What is going to be your legacy?" My answer was simple. "I do not have a legacy unless my successor is successful." Two years later, as I write this book, I am confident I can say, "Mission accomplished." Muhtar and I set out to make the transition seamless, something that proved difficult to say the least in many previous ones.

Each time I see Coke board members, they thank me for the smooth transition. Thanks to Muhtar, I am not one of the many embittered former CEOs. I have no disappointment in what I achieved or what I left behind. I regretted that I did not complete the CCE merger, but Muhtar did, and the company will reap great dividends from that in the future. It's very comforting to see the company in such capable hands.

Pamela and I are both different people after the five years at the helm of Coke; both more outwardly focused than we were before. My first retirement was more of a normal retirement, taking it easy and playing golf and traveling. Now I am much more involved in world affairs, serving on a number of boards, including the World Wildlife Fund, General Motors, the Investment Climate Facility for Africa, and DGM Bank in Barbados, from which I also run my investment company.

In the fall of 2007, Rick Wagoner, then Chairman and CEO of General Motors, and George Fisher, the lead director, approached me about joining the board of GM. Rick came to visit me in Atlanta and my driver met him at the airport to take him to dinner with me. The car was a Ford. I was well aware of that as Coca-Cola was a Ford customer, a legacy of Roberto Goizueta's long tenure on the Ford board. I could have arranged for a GM car and hidden the fact that I drove around in a competitor's products or let the facts speak for themselves. It was the beginning of a brief relationship with Rick. I only joined the GM board in August of 2008 as I did not feel like I could devote the time I needed to until I handed over the job of CEO of Coca-Cola to Muhtar.

The saga of GM is well documented so I will not take a chapter of this book to write about it. Suffice it to say that the journey from August 2008 to today has encompassed some of the most fascinating and stressful moments of my business life.

I do feel Rick has been criticized unfairly in many quarters. I believe that he achieved a great deal within the framework of the "art of the possible." However, he did not manage to reform the bureaucratic culture of the old GM—a huge task, as at least forty years of layering by committees and internal boards meant a lack of accountability and a slow decision-making process. With the financial meltdown, the task clearly became nearly impossible and much as we tried to avoid bankruptcy, eventually only the government, on its terms, could save GM. That Rick's resignation was demanded by President Obama was initially something I felt was wrong and yet I had to recognize that the new majority owner had the right to demand this. I also had to cross a philosophical bridge regarding government ownership of a private company. This was a black swan event and there is no question in my mind today that it was not only the right decision for GM but also for the U.S. economy. Exceptions sometimes trump rules, for the rules are drawn for more normal parameters.

I joined GM because it is an iconic company like Coca-Cola and I am proud to serve on its board today after the trauma of bankruptcy. Clearly, the massive change which GM needed has been significantly enabled by the leadership of Ed Whitaker and now Dan Akerson.

The mission is simple: design, build, and sell the world's best cars. No mention of market share, global leadership, or even profit margins. Fulfill the mission and everything falls into its correct bucket.

One final comment. The new generation of great cars now appearing predate the bankruptcy. The hiring of Bob Lutz by Rick Wagoner was a real shock to its system. Bob is a "car guy, not a bean counter," as he puts it. He assembled a great team with visionary designers led by Ed Welburn. There is still a great deal to do but Akerson can be proud of the new GM.

On the philanthropic side of my second retirement, Pamela and I, along with investment banker Chris Flowers, formed a foundation to fight malaria in Africa, with a program in Zambia to distribute mosquito nets coated with insecticide.

The passion that I have for these causes, the Coca-Cola Company, and what it stands for is shared by my family members, who are also my greatest critics. After a speech which I felt was good and which receives positive audience response,

Pamela will bring me back to earth with very productive comments about what I did wrong. My family members are my conscience as well and nothing defines that better than when Cara asked me after viewing some of the Coca-Cola Christmas polar bear commercials, which she loved, "Dad, what are you doing for the polar bears?" The answer, frankly, was very little. From this has grown a major program, focused on the plight of the polar bear, which Coca-Cola launched with the World Wildlife Fund, a program which Muhtar has a passion for and will result after the publication of this book in a spectacular Christmas program. The Isdell Family Foundation also sponsors Bear Trek, an innovative bear awareness and protection program. I now look at companies that use threatened species to promote their products and ask what they are doing to help their plight. Cara made me think differently. Film stars have agents. Should animals not have them too?

Toward the end of my time as Chairman and CEO, I began giving speeches about my vision for capitalism, based on my experiences around the world through so many pivotal points in history. I call it "Connected Capitalism."

Eight

CONNECTED CAPITALISM

A biracial group of Atlanta civic and religious leaders planned a celebratory dinner for Martin Luther King Jr. after he was awarded the Nobel Peace Prize in late 1964. King became only the second Nobel laureate from the Southern U.S., the first being the writer William Faulkner.

The dinner was to be held January 27, 1965, at the Dinkler Plaza Hotel in downtown Atlanta. Yet there were soon press reports that Atlanta's business community planned to snub King, in part because after returning from the Nobel acceptance ceremony in Oslo, he had briefly joined the picket line at Scripto, a ballpoint pen manufacturing plant in Atlanta where union workers were on strike for higher wages and an end to racial discrimination in job classifications.

"Banquet for Dr. King Meets Obstacles Here," read the *Atlanta Journal* headline on December 29, 1964.

Robert W. Woodruff had then retired from the day-to-day operations of Coca-Cola but still very much controlled the

company behind the scenes. The banquet organizing commit-
tee, which included a Catholic archbishop, Paul Hallinan, Rabbi
Jacob Rothschild, Morehouse College President Benjamin
Mays, and *Atlanta Constitution* publisher Ralph McGill, wrote
Woodruff on December 16, asking to use his name on the din-
ner invitations as one of the event's hundred sponsors.

Woodruff did not immediately respond, prompting a follow-up letter on December 29, the same day the *Atlanta Journal*
reported "obstacles" in generating support for the banquet.

In a draft letter written from his Ichauway Plantation in
South Georgia, Woodruff replied that "I will be glad to be one
of the one hundred Atlanta citizens serving as a sponsoring
group for this recognition dinner." Boisieuillet Jones, who ran
the Emily and Ernest Woodruff Foundation, wrote a similar
letter of support that same day. Both letters are now housed
among Woodruff's papers at Emory University's Manuscript,
Archives, and Rare Book Library in Atlanta.

Suddenly, Atlanta's attitude about the dinner changed dramatically.

"All Tickets Gone for King Dinner," read an *Atlanta Constitution* headline on January 21, 1965. In a complete turnaround,
more than one thousand tickets were sold.

Woodruff "politely persuaded" the Atlanta business community to support the event, recalled Sam Massell, then the city's
vice mayor, who attended the banquet and was seated at the
front table. "It would not have come off if it had not been for
Mr. Woodruff," Massell said.

Clearly, Woodruff realized that a no-show at the banquet
would have been a worldwide embarrassment for Coca-Cola
and for Atlanta.

"It was of mutual interest to have the dinner," said Massell, who later was elected mayor of Atlanta.

The night of the dinner, King delivered to a standing-room-only, integrated audience what would become one of his most famous quotes: "If the people of good will of the white South fail to act now, history will have to record that the greatest tragedy of this period of social transition was not the vitriolic words and the violent actions of the bad people but the appalling silence of and indifference of the good people."

All segments of Atlanta society were there: churches and synagogues, government, private universities and business, all working together, as Massell recalled, for their "mutual interest." That is Connected Capitalism.

Woodruff and Coca-Cola quietly asserted moral leadership, knowing that it was not simply the right thing to do but that it would also benefit the company. Woodruff was a visionary who had expanded Coca-Cola worldwide and realized that its success transcended quarterly profit statements. Long-term success for Coca-Cola demanded that it take a strong moral leadership role in its hometown, extending outward from that base.

Paul Austin, Coke's CEO from 1966 to 1981, was also a visionary. A Harvard-educated lawyer who competed as a rower in the 1936 Olympics in Berlin, Austin believed Coca-Cola had an obligation to fight world hunger. He created the company's "Nutrition Project" that developed three protein-rich drinks, Saci, Samson, and Tai, made from soy and whey, which were sold in South America and Africa.

As a young Coke employee in Zambia in the 1960s, I participated in a trial run of Saci. I was very enthusiastic about the project, seeing it as a way for Coca-Cola to make a big dent in world hunger in a commercial/humanitarian/government joint effort. I soon realized, however, there were a few problems. Saci was too expensive and there was no way we could make a profit. We did the test on a subsidized basis, hoping in the future to find a lower cost. That never happened because another lesson was learned: It tasted awful and no one wanted to drink it. It clung to your pallet and had a terrible aftertaste. Something may be good for you but if it doesn't taste good you're not going to consume it. We would distribute it to schools and other locations and even when handed out free of charge, it wasn't consumed. Decades later as CEO, I explored the possibility that new technology would allow us to create a similar product with a better flavor but it didn't work. Despite its flaws, Austin believed that the program was morally correct and good for business in the long term and deserves credit for making the effort.

Austin also realized that water would continue to be a worldwide issue for Coca-Cola. The company under his leadership purchased Aqua-Chem, which makes equipment to remove salt from seawater. Although Coca-Cola sold Aqua-Chem in 1981, Austin was clearly decades ahead of his time in putting Coca-Cola on an environmentally sustainable path. He realized that Coca-Cola could not simply extract profits, it had to improve the societies in which its customers lived. Critics argued that these efforts were diversions from Coca-Cola's core business mission, and from a business standpoint, they are correct. Yet unlike Coke's purchase of Columbia Pictures, Austin's efforts were motivated by larger issues than profit alone. He believed that Coca-Cola had the ability to become a major player in the fight to clean the planet and fight world hunger. In that regard, he was prescient.

"The more money we make, the less welcome we become," Austin wrote to Woodruff in 1970. When I read that quote, I can't help but remember Maurice Gersh, the Coca-Cola bottler in Zambia who first hired me shortly after I graduated from college. Gersh was not only the Coke bottler in Kitwe, but was also the town's mayor. It must have been very difficult for anyone in Kitwe to feel as if Coca-Cola was a strange, foreign company unwelcome in their town when the mayor himself was a franchisee. That kind of connectivity eliminates corporate estrangement. A company can't easily hide from society and its problems when the two are so closely melded.

In order to remain economically competitive, Coca-Cola and many other companies have by necessity consolidated many of these small outposts which had those strong and vital ties to the community. I think back to Germany, where I devoted much time and energy whittling down the number of bottlers from more than a hundred to one. It had to be done if Coke was to remain competitive as a company. The small bottlers were built at a time when capital was hard to come by, most stores were small, and transportation costs were higher because there were fewer major highways and many bridges had been destroyed during the war. With the advent of supermarkets and interstate highways, small bottlers no longer made economic sense and threatened Coca-Cola's ability to offer low-cost, profitable products. The reason that the cost of Coke, when adjusted for inflation, is lower now than it was decades ago is directly re-lated to the higher efficiency achieved through bottler con-solidation.

While consolidation was necessary, I regret that we lost the connection the bottlers had with their local communities. These connections were so strong that even the promise of millions in extra profit was not enough to convince some German bottlers to sell their plants. It was prestigious to be *the* Coca-Cola bottler in your community and with that prestige was the obligation to be a civic and moral leader.

The question now is: Within today's global corporate structure, what are the opportunities for the modern-day equivalent of Maurice Gersh? They are actually far greater than they were in Maurice's time. As the mayor of Kitwe and the local bottler, he had strong ties to the community but did not have the chance to participate in the much larger, sweeping campaigns of today, such as a worldwide fight against malaria, restoring critical watersheds, or helping mango farmers in Haiti following a devastating earthquake.

Today, a corporate executive can do this and much more. It is Connected Capitalism on a much larger scale.

The corporate leader of yesterday worked closely with government and nonprofits on a local level. There were civic clubs and fund-raising drives for new hospitals and other worthy causes. Today's equivalent might be partnerships with the World Wildlife Fund or the United Nations. The project could be a local hospital or one thousand miles away in Africa. So the corporate options for affecting major change are actually far greater than they were in the time of Maurice Gersh. I was trained in college to be a social worker, yet chose a path in business. As corporations evolved, I had a far greater opportunity at Coca-Cola to affect true social change globally than I ever would have as a social worker in Africa. Capitalism now provides that opportunity. No longer are the lines drawn so distinctly.

Much has been written about Corporate Social Responsibility, a movement which has motivated companies to do many great things. My vision for Connected Capitalism advocates going much further to create a melding, a true marriage between government, nonprofits, and global corporations to fight disease and poverty, heal the planet, improve education, and, ultimately, boost private-sector profits.

Corporate Social Responsibility sometimes involves a "pet project," singled out by the CEO or the CEO's spouse. These are often worthy projects, but not always directly linked to the company's core business strategy or the impact the business has on society. Connected Capitalism is much broader. It is the creation of the Socially Responsible Corporation, which examines the company's actual footprint on society and focuses on how, as part of a core business strategy, it can reduce the negative impact. If you are making a profit through excessive use or extraction of the world's resources, you have an issue that needs to be addressed. You have to become a better caretaker of those resources. It's in the best interest of the shareholders and of society to do so. A clear example is that neither Coca-Cola nor the communities where it operates can survive for long without adequate water. Their destinies are directly linked. That is why Coca-Cola now has a vice president for environment and water resources. Jeff Seabright currently holds this high-profile position; at one time he worked in the White House as executive director of the Climate Change Task Force and helped negotiate the Kyoto Protocol.

The term "corporate social responsibility" carries with it a slight tone of penance, almost as if companies owe society a debt for making a profit. That is not really the core issue. There should be no shame in making a profit as long is it earned in a socially responsible way. In my career, I saw how Coca-Cola pulled millions of people out of poverty throughout the world when other efforts had failed. Afghanistan is one telling example.

In 2006, when I was Chairman and CEO, Coca-Cola opened a $25 million bottling plant in Kabul, creating 350 jobs. A critic said the $25 million would have been better spent on a hospital. My question was this: Without jobs, without businesses, how would the hospital be able to sustain itself? Where would the money come from to pay the doctors and maintain the building?

A thriving Coca-Cola bottling plant can help support that hospital through donations and through taxes paid by the company, its employees, and its vendors. With jobs, workers can afford to pay for medical treatment. Without capitalism, the hospital would rely forever on handouts, an unsustainable model.

As the three key elements of the triangle of sustainability—business, nonprofits, and governments—work more closely together in the future, there should be an acknowledgment of the strengths each brings to the table. Business brings efficiency and profit, and that is not something of which we should be ashamed.

People are often amazed at how Coca-Cola manages to deliver its products to the most remote locations of the world. I remember in Zambia, vendors would load cases of Coke in dugout canoes and row deep into the wilderness where they would post a Coca-Cola sign and sell cold drinks.

The secret to the Coca-Cola distribution method is that everyone along the way, from start to finish, makes a profit. It may be a tiny profit, but it is a profit nonetheless and that drives efficiency. Tom Mattia, who worked for me as a senior vice president when I was CEO, once tracked a case of Coke in Kenya from start to finish.

"The last transaction was a goat," he recalled. "They traded a baby goat for a case of Coke."

In March 2011, Melinda Gates visited a Coca-Cola micro-distribution center in Nairobi specifically to learn how the strengths of the company's system could be applied in the health-care field. She was amazed with the efficiency of the operation and Coke's use of real-time data. The sales staff in the field relays orders by text message to the distribution center and the information is stored in a database. "What lessons from this incredible data gathering could we apply to health care?" Melinda asked in a blog posting about the trip. "There are lessons to be learned from every sector, and we need to be willing to look far and wide for solutions to the challenges we face in health and development."

So many efforts by nonprofits involve distributing food, vaccines, and other vital supplies to the world's most remote locations. Can companies like Coke, with their unequalled distribution systems, help in this effort? Yes. Could they do it "free"? Yes, but that is not a sustainable model. One that would work over the long term would be to develop a system that involves a profit for everyone in the chain. Could the men in the dugout canoes in Zambia also deliver condoms and medicine? Perhaps, and they could likely make the delivery at a fraction of the cost of a stand-alone delivery system. First, however, we have to embrace business as part of the three-way partnership, recognizing and respecting what business is and what it does. A business is not by definition a philanthropic entity, nor should it be, but is striving in its own interest to be a generator of long-term sustainable profits.

Corporations, therefore, are like any other organism: They have to operate sustainably if they are to last. Coca-Cola has been in business for 125 years. If it's to last for another 125 years, it has to maintain a business strategy that is sustainable over the long term. You, the reader, have seen in this book the many trials and tribulations of a modern corporation, the extreme pressure to remain competitive, and how quickly companies can fall apart. Think back to the comment from David Rubenstein, the investment banker, when Coke's market cap had dropped to $96 billion: "Well, that's a bit out of our reach, for now," he said. If a corporation allows its stock price to dip too low, and becomes the target of a leveraged buyout, it loses control of its own future and risks being broken up and sold in parts. If that happens, the corporation ends up having to fight for its life, as opposed to assisting in the fight against malaria or AIDS or preserving critical water basins. Extreme corporate critics wonder why we don't simply donate most if not at all of our profits to the world's great causes. The reason is simply because we would not be around for long if we did so.

In my vision of Connected Capitalism, you have both higher profits and progress. The two do not conflict. In fact, one demands the other.

Obviously, corporate profits increase over the long term if unemployment rates drop from 50 percent—the current number in many countries—to even 25 percent. If the population is healthier and more educated, yes, companies make more money and can do even more to improve society. Remember that in disease-ravaged countries, local companies also suffer from the dire consequences of epidemics, losing valuable employees to such illnesses as AIDS and malaria. Companies have a direct and vested interest in the fight against such diseases.

There are many other immediate benefits from capitalism that is connected.

Tom Mattia recalled a bottler in Africa who, realizing that the local villagers were getting sick from drinking water out of a polluted river, decided to drill two wells. The cost was equal to a one-way ticket from Johannesburg to Atlanta, Tom said. Besides being used for drinking, the well water was also used to irrigate crops. As a result of the wells, sickness declined and farm income increased. And as the community's fortunes improved, so did sales of Coca-Cola. It was a perfect example of Connected Capitalism.

Governments and nonprofits should approach corporate partnerships with this type of thinking. Companies should not be considered as passive partners, simply writing checks which they can then tout in their annual reports and press releases. Just as corporations should begin to think more like nonprofits, so nonprofits should think more like businesses. They should look for opportunities that will allow companies to both increase profit and improve the world. This is not just about money. It's about skills, engagement, and intellectual capital.

Only when companies are financially healthy and moving in an upward trajectory can they seriously engage in long-term partnerships. If an NGO had approached Coca-Cola in the early days of my tenure as CEO, they would have come across a different, far more stressed version of myself than in the later years, when we did expand major partnerships. In the early days, my focus was on righting the ship. Only later, when these efforts proved successful, could I seriously entertain the notion of expanding the company's involvement in projects such as digging wells. The point is that corporations have to succeed before they can help others. The adage, "To do good, you must do well," is entirely accurate. It is vital for NGOs to understand that and to approach corporations with ideas and proposals that are designed with this in mind.

The best corporate partnerships, in fact the only sustainable ones, are those which are focused on a company's core business. For Coca-Cola, the most important issue is water, since that is a key ingredient in all of our products. It was not difficult even for stock analysts to understand the relevance and importance of spending millions of dollars on this issue. When challenged at an analysts meeting, all I had to do was hold up a can of Coke to illustrate the importance of that key ingredient. I was never challenged again. Our bottlers also clearly understand how crucial these efforts are. CCHBC, the European bottler I once ran, has worked to preserve the Danube River. Why? The river runs through most of the countries in the CCHBC territory.

Once a company has established partnerships in its core area, it can then begin expanding to other related areas. For example, Coca-Cola joined a partnership called Nets for Life, which brings together corporations, foundations, NGOs, and faith-based organizations to distribute insecticide-coated mosquito nets in the most remote locations of Africa. Following my retirement, I launched a similar effort in Zambia along with investment banker Christopher Flowers; we serve an area of the country not covered by Nets for Life.

Under the old model of corporate philanthropy, NGOs would approach companies, seeking only cash. Usually, the philanthropic department of a corporation was a small, separate unit divorced from the company's day-to-day business operations.

The new model is much different, as Carter Roberts, president of the World Wildlife Fund explains. Today, NGOs like the WWF work with the world's largest corporations and their suppliers to help and encourage them to use less energy, water, and land, and to reduce carbon emissions as part of a long-term business strategy that will ultimately improve profits. "It's not about throwing a little bit of money at an NGO or an environmental group," Carter said.

The old-fashioned environmental community looked at corporations more as enemies than partners, said Carter. Under the new model, that is changing. Carter himself has an MBA from Harvard and formerly worked for big corporations such as Proctor & Gamble. He understands that there are business leaders who also believe in protecting the planet and are incorporating steps to do so in their business models. "I've always said that these partnerships really don't work unless I can look the CEO in the eye and know that they are committed at the highest levels," said Carter.

Corporate efforts on behalf of the environment are producing real results. In late 2010, the Consumer Goods Forum, cochaired by Muhtar, pledged to begin phasing out hydrofluorocarbon refrigerants as of 2015 and to achieve zero net deforestation by 2020, all in an effort to fight climate change. The forum's members include the world's largest corporations, among them Walmart, General Mills, and Johnson & Johnson.

In the long term, corporations will benefit from these efforts because they will become increasingly efficient, developing methods and technology that will allow them to consume less of the world's natural resources, which are becoming increasingly scarce, Carter said.

"We have a finite planet," Carter said. "We have to meet the needs of a population that is going to grow to nine billion people. Something has to give. A big part of that is becoming more efficient."

NGOs, while partnering with corporations, are by no means their shills, Carter explained. They reserve the right to publicly complain when companies don't deliver on their promises. NGOs, like corporations, have to preserve the credibility of their own brands. The NGOs ensure that corporations keep their side of the bargain. At the same time, NGOs realize that corporations are not philanthropic entities, and must make a profit if they are to remain engaged in these global efforts.

"We want the good guys to prosper," said Carter.

The partnerships are not always easy to maintain. Organizations are run by humans, and all the normal human conflicts, egos, and pride come into play.

My first detailed involvement with an NGO which endorsed the many germinal thoughts I had about business and society working together was when the Coca-Cola Company asked me in 1995 to join the Prince of Wales International Business Leaders Forum. It was founded in Charleston, South Carolina, in 1990, shortly after the Exxon *Valdez* oil spill. The organization was inspired by the vision of Prince Charles together with the visionary Robert Davies, who led the organization for many years and was to become a good friend of mine. IBLF was a new model and a breakout model. It promotes corporate profitability and community sustainability at the same time, acknowledging that the two do not have to conflict.

I left the IBLF board when I retired the first time in 2001 but returned after much persuasion to chair the board in 2006 after I had returned to Coca-Cola. Sadly, Robert Davies fell ill and died the following year. What had been for me a role of supporting a dynamic leader and attending two board meetings a year—one with Prince Charles—became a very stressful experience, as I was then Chairman and CEO of the Coca-Cola Company.

Robert had presented to the board a new logo design which reduced the profile of the words "Prince of Wales." He'd convinced us that the change came with the blessing of the prince and that he was happy for the IBLF to start taking a more independent route. I was later told by another participant in a meeting with the prince that this was not, in fact, the case. At the same time, the private secretary of the prince had begun an exercise in examining the many disparate organizations the prince had founded, not only to allow the prince to focus more closely on his philanthropic enterprises, but also to improve the profile of the extensive interests and commitment he displayed. I attended a few workshops with leaders of the other organizations and an effective model was developing.

I was shocked, however, to receive a letter from the prince saying he wanted to merge the IBLF with Business in the Community, an organization he'd founded in the United Kingdom that promotes corporate social responsibility. The IBLF had been split off from Business in the Community when it was decided they were very different organizations. They still were very different. IBLF operates solely outside the UK in developing markets and has a somewhat rural focus, working with major multinational companies. Business in the Community was

UK based and mostly urban, with a medium-sized industry base. One of the issues with merging the groups was that some of the UK-based companies were members of both organizations; a merger would obviously significantly reduce revenues since those companies would not pay the fees twice.

The prince was determined to make the merger happen. In the meeting I had with him and a further one with the head of the board of trustees of Business in the Community, Sir Stuart Rose, then the executive chairman of retailer Marks & Spencer, I achieved an agreement to have a major consulting firm evaluate the proposal. The study clearly showed that the financial risks were too great and that the original logic for separate organizations still held. The operating head of Business in the Community, who would ultimately run the merged organization, told me he could not disagree with the study but still believed that the merger should take place. It was clear the prince's office was applying a great deal of pressure on him to complete what I believed was, in fact, a takeover. I thought, however, that I had the support of Sir Stuart, who endorsed the study in a meeting at his office and stated that he would support the recommendation. A week later, Sir Stuart phoned me to say he had changed his mind.

There was additional tension with the prince: His office opposed the person selected by the IBLF search committee to succeed Robert Davies; I endorsed the candidate. The IBLF board went ahead and appointed him anyway, despite the prince's objection, which was fully within their rights since the trustees had complete oversight of the charity and not the prince. However, it had been customary for the prince to give his nod on major decisions. As we disagreed this time, it made for another unhappy meeting with Prince Charles. During my last formal meeting with the prince, he told me his "wishes" were that the merger take place. I told him my board of trustees could not vote for it. There was a rather chilly and formal farewell and a few weeks later a letter arrived in which Prince Charles informed me he was withdrawing his patronage. We were now the International Leaders Business Forum; no Prince of Wales. This, I believe in retrospect, is where Robert Davies was headed, but I would not have supported him as I still favored Prince Charles's involvement. My opposition to the merger, as I tried to point out to the prince, was something I believed passionately was in his interest. For me to have agreed would have been very easy. With all that I had on my plate at Coca-Cola, one less involvement would have been welcomed. Opposing the merger also ate up a large amount of my time and was an unwelcome diversion.

The prince, in my view, is very well meaning and while I do not agree with him on every issue, he continues to be seen as being ahead of his time particularly on environmental issues. However, he is a future king, very strong willed, and very used to getting his own way. Those surrounding him are evaluated on how they meet his needs and in my view do not always challenge him enough. The old ways of the court still hold. I suppose I should also say that I have a stubborn streak myself, so ours was a relationship in which two wills collided. Needless to say, my Christmas card from the prince is no more.

I take no pleasure in this story in that the struggle to keep the identity of the IBLF was difficult. Some members left as a result of the removal of the royal patronage but the situation has since stabilized. In 2011 I handed over the leadership to Mark Foster, who works in London; I'd found it difficult to manage the organization from the distance of Barbados. In retrospect, the biggest and most stressful point in my tenure at IBLF—which really complicated everything—was that Robert Davies's replacement, whom I supported, did not work out. On that issue, the prince had been right and I had been wrong.

What's the message from the previous story? In high-profile, high-stakes partnerships, conflicts come with the territory, and you *must* be able to get through them *without* jeopardizing the greater mission.

Often, the partnerships that address climate change and other broad issues are large and extensive. Then there are the much smaller—but also very important—efforts that connect companies, NGOs, and government, many of which do not involve money at all.

Just as NGOs and governments have large toolboxes of knowledge and expertise, so do corporations. In the marriage that is Connected Capitalism, these assets should be shared by the partners. Companies can help nonprofits and smaller community-based businesses with technology, supply-chain management, marketing and distribution, and employee training.

One of the most interesting cases illustrating this involves CARE, the Atlanta-based international relief organization, and United Parcel Service Inc.

For years, UPS donated cash to CARE, a passive form of help when you stop and realize that CARE distributes relief supplies around the world, and UPS, which operates in more than two hundred countries, is the world's largest package delivery company. In 2007, a CARE executive, Rigoberto Giron, asked UPS to help the agency with logistics. Giron has a business background and understands the value of what UPS could offer. After all, NGOs, just like corporations, have to remain efficient and competitive. They are competing for donors' dollars, just as Coca-Cola is competing for the dollars of consumers.

Two UPS executives, Dale Herzog and Jim Coughlan, started the partnership by visiting CARE offices in Honduras, Darfur, and Indonesia. CARE allowed UPS executives full access to its operations, an unusual openness that at the same time drew the two organizations closer together. Herzog discovered that CARE had no computerized database of its supplies, which were stored all over the world. Instead, each CARE office maintained its own inventory list on spreadsheets which were located on the hard drives of individual computers. Herzog also found that CARE needed to expand the scope of its centralized purchasing system for supplies such as tents and bottled water. The agency had no program for prepositioning those supplies throughout the world so that they could be transported more easily to disaster sites. More troubling to Herzog was the fact that CARE had very little unrestricted funding that could be used, not for a particular disaster such as an earthquake in Haiti but to increase the company's long-term efficiency. For example, CARE had little money to buy supplies at volume discounts, long before a disaster hit, which would have lowered costs tremendously since prices of supplies always jump immediately following a catastrophe.

Donors, however, normally want their money sent directly to the disaster they are watching unfold on their television screens. It's harder to raise funds for longer-term projects.

With help from Aidmatrix, a Texas-based NGO, Herzog and CARE developed a computer system that would allow it to track supplies worldwide in real time. UPS has also donated money to Aidmatrix. CARE's new database was tested in Sri Lanka and Haiti and is now being rolled out worldwide.

Herzog and CARE are expanding the centralized purchasing system. "Why would I have seventy countries buying fifteen Toyotas each when you could buy all of them at one time and maybe get a bigger discount?" asked Herzog.

Interestingly, as CARE and UPS worked together in a partnership that was not centered around money, the relationship strengthened and UPS increased its cash donation from $200,000 a year to $1 million. That is the power of engagement. Some of the extra dollars will go toward the prepositioning of relief supplies deemed so important but at the same time so difficult to fund through donor dollars.

How does UPS benefit from its connections with CARE? It is now deeply involved in the humanitarian relief arena, which is constantly shipping supplies worldwide. "There are billions of dollars of freight moved and maybe 10 percent of the shipping is donated," said Herzog. "There is a corporate citizenship within UPS that just wants to do what's right. We can help people in ways that many people can't. There's also a commercial aspect of this. It's a large space that UPS has not been in."

It is reasonable to expect that as UPS builds its reputation in the humanitarian relief community through its work with CARE that UPS's profits will also increase. And its profits are being used to help fund CARE. The relationship is circular, a wonderful example of Connected Capitalism. And like all successful partnerships, it continues to grow.

Currently, the partners are working on a paperless distribution system for relief supplies. When the UPS delivery man or woman knocks on your door with a package, you sign an electronic keypad, not a piece of paper. It saves an enormous amount of time, money, and paper. UPS and CARE have tested similar devices in Haiti and Bangladesh for the delivery of relief supplies.

"It's a natural evolution of efficiency," said Herzog. "We are bringing good, sound business practices into an area that in many cases is devoid of those."

Step back for a moment and consider what is happening with this partnership. The giant corporation is becoming more like an NGO. The NGO is becoming more like a corporation. Both are better organizations from the connection.

The dollars CARE saves through efficiency can be used to expand its services. At the same time, donors can be assured that CARE is using its money effectively, with help from one of the world's most efficient corporations. This interrelationship illustrates how we are evolving from an atmosphere of extreme distrust between corporations and NGOs to a relationship that is mutually beneficial, one in which there are fewer and fewer barriers.

One fringe benefit is the effect on employee morale. It's invigorating for corporate executives to donate their time and expertise to NGOS. "Everybody wants my job," said Herzog, laughing. Partnerships between corporations and NGOs indeed help companies recruit the best and brightest. No longer does the idealistic college graduate necessarily have to choose between a career in business or one at an NGO. The lines are blurring and rightly so.

Corporations want to help and NGOs might be surprised at the enthusiasm these partnerships generate within the business community. Derrick Kayongo, a CARE executive originally from Uganda, was shocked when he came to the United States and saw that soap in hotel rooms was tossed into the trash each day by the cleaning crews, even though the expensive bars were only slightly used. In Uganda, soap was a scarce commodity, yet hotels in the U.S. were tossing tons of it into the garbage daily. Kayongo spoke before a group of Atlanta hotel executives and asked them to donate their slightly used soap to a nonprofit group he established called the Global Soap Project, which would recycle it and ship it to Africa.

The response was overwhelming. Hotels realized they could save money on landfill costs by recycling the soap instead of discarding it. At the same time they could engage their employees in a program to help reduce disease in the developing world. The Soap Project has now collected fifty tons of used soap from all over the U.S., not just Atlanta. After reading about the project in a news story, one Boston hotel shipped a ton of soap to Atlanta. The Soap Project has partnered with other NGOs, such as Medshare, to ship the soap to Africa, Haiti, and other places where soap is in short supply. A Virginia for-profit company, Relief Cargo, paid $2,700 for one 1,400-pound shipment of soap to Kenya.

The Soap Project is also exploring social entrepreneurship opportunities, possibly to fund its operations in part by selling the recycled soap to governments for use in jails.

Social entrepreneurship is another rapidly emerging field that uses profit to help solve problems in the developing world. These companies are investing in microfinance and the development of small companies in India and other countries. One such company is d.light. Born in a Stanford University classroom, the company produces low-cost solar-powered lanterns, marketing the products to the hundreds of millions of people in the world without electricity. The benefits are wide-ranging and obvious: The lights are safer than kerosene lanterns, thus reducing the risk of fire and toxic fumes. There is a strong educational component as well: Children have more time to study at night. Poultry farmers are even using the solar lights to increase egg production. D.light is very much a for-profit company, funded in part by venture capitalists in the U.S., but it also reaches out to NGOs for donations to help those who can't afford to buy the lights. We are seeing these types of business interactions all over the world.

Another Indian startup, PharmaSecure, has developed a system for battling counterfeit prescription drugs, a huge and dangerous problem in India. This company, founded by a Dartmouth College graduate, Nathan Sigworth, and also funded by venture capitalists, created a system that allows pharmaceutical companies to include a unique code with each prescription. The customer can then use their mobile phone to text that code to a phone number printed next to the code. The customer receives a reply text message to let them know whether the medicine is authentic. The system not only saves lives and reduces counterfeiting but provides pharmaceutical companies with a way to distinguish their brands from competitors.

Capitalism, of course, has its faults. There are good corporations and bad ones, just as there are good governments and corrupt ones, effective NGOs and ineffective ones. Yet it's capitalism that is allowing companies like PharmaSecure and d.light to actually change the developing world for the better, in real, tangible ways. These companies sometimes work with the help of NGOs, but the most powerful engine of the change they strive to effect is capitalism. Why capitalism? Why did these entrepreneurs embrace the for-profit model rather than simply create their own NGOs and raise donations from the corporate world for their worthy causes?

Dorcas Cheng-Tozun, a spokeswoman for d.light, summarizes the answer in two words: sustainability and scalability. Donations come and go, but if a company is well-run, profits will be always be there and will sustain the effort over the long term. With 1.6 billion people in the world living without electricity, private investment capital made it much faster for d.light to attack the problem broadly and quickly, Cheng-Tozun said.

"NGOs have been trying to address this for a quite a number of years now and have done the best they could with the resources they had," she said. "Really, no nonprofit organization that is addressing lighting in the developing world has been able to scale. They are able to do little projects here and there with maybe one village or a few hundred homes, and then they run out of money. We really felt like that if we wanted to address this need on a global scale, at a level at which we could actually make an impact, we need a business model to be sustainable, to not rely on donation dollars and to be scalable."

Investment capital allowed the company to launch very quickly and to build a factory in China to produce lanterns in large volume, which allowed an economy of scale that then makes the product less expensive. The company opened sales offices in

India and Tanzania within a few months of its launch in 2008. In less than three years of operation, d.light has served three million customers.

Selling the lanterns rather than giving them away also changes the dynamic with the customer in a positive way, Cheng-Tozun added. "When you have an NGO that is providing free services or even very heavily subsidized services, then the customers become passive recipients," she said. "Our customers are empowered. We need to give them exactly the kind of products that they need and want and are willing to pay for. If we don't make the products they want, they are going to vote with their dollars. We provide warranties on our products. We have customer service lines. We have centers set up so that if they have a problem with our products, they can come in and get it fixed or exchange it. We feel like that is a much healthier dynamic than if we were an NGO."

D.light does work with NGOs to distribute lanterns for disaster relief and in areas where the people are simply too poor to buy them. Yet the majority of the company's sales are through open-market channels.

I have included the story of d.light not to denigrate in any way the great work that NGOs are doing throughout the world, but only to illustrate that capitalism can also work wonders, particularly when companies and NGOs combine their efforts.

Governments, however, are in many cases lagging behind corporations and nonprofits in forging partnerships. Many governments still believe that the way to solve problems is simply to pass more laws. They have not learned that the most effective strategy is to work together with business and NGOs to develop programs that benefit all three parties.

That is starting to change. I cochair along with Benjamin Mkapa, former president of Tanzania, a nonprofit group called the Investment Climate Facility for Africa. It is a partnership with business and government to improve the investment climate in Africa and foster business growth. It is working. I have witnessed the results of the effort firsthand.

You can now register a business in Rwanda in one day. Instead of registering four or five businesses a day, as was the case, Rwanda is now registering seventy. It's a one-stop shop, and you can also register your business online.

We have also worked to improve commercial courts of law in Africa so that businesses can have a fast, efficient venue for resolving disputes. We have helped governments convert their courts from paper to digital technology, increasing accuracy and speed and greatly reducing backlogs.

A land transfer in Burkina Faso once required something like seventeen signatures. It now requires only seven.

These are examples of accomplishments that can be duplicated around the world with partnerships, with Connected Capitalism.

Critics will point to disasters such as the British Petroleum oil spill in the Gulf of Mexico in 2010 as an example of how capitalism is rapacious and puts profits above the planet and all else. BP, after all, was big on sustainability. It spent billions to promote low-carbon alternatives to oil such as biofuels and wind power.

Yet the benefits of those efforts and a company's credibility can be wiped out instantly with a major mistake such as the Gulf oil spill. Connected Capitalism is not a front that forgives all other corporate sins. The compact demands that all participants—government, NGOs, and business—act responsibly or the partnership will collapse. Acting responsibly is also something that corporations must do to ensure their own long-term survival and the survival of the capitalist system that allows them to flourish.

BP and its stockholders paid dearly for the oil spill, both financially and in the damage to the brand. The mistake played directly into the hands of those who oppose capitalism and are looking for any excuse to attack it. Companies have to be seen as adding value to society. Otherwise, you have populist politicians who stand up and do what Hugo Chávez did in Venezuela. The reason there is a Chávez is that the business leaders in Venezuela were essentially robber barons. They did not have enough connection to the people to prompt them to stand up to Chávez when he began nationalizing industry and destroying the capitalist system, all the while giving citizens the false promise of nirvana. Cuba was the same, and there are many other examples. Frankly, it would have been difficult to find many people to stand up in support of BP after the Gulf oil spill. In fact, some prominent people, including former U.S. Labor Secretary Robert Reich, called for the U.S. to take over BP's operations in the Gulf in the form of a temporary receivership.

When I retired as Chairman of Coca-Cola in 2009, the world seemed to be giving up on capitalism. Banks and other major industries were collapsing and some were effectively nationalized. "We are all socialists now," *Newsweek* declared in February 2009.

In a lifetime of traveling the world, I have seen socialism and communism at work, and they don't work. I have seen the gray landscape in East Germany before the Wall fell, and shelves so barren I had difficulty finding anything to buy. In Russia I have seen the system that could not even produce paper cups for soda machines and the mind-set of well-meaning and hardworking citizens who yearned for a better life for themselves and their children but were so beaten down by the system that their talents and energy were largely wasted. I have also seen socialism's toll on my beloved Africa.

If capitalism fails, it will be because, we, the capitalists, have let the people down. It will happen only if we allow our companies to become disconnected from the societies they serve.

In the future, corporations will increasingly be judged not only by customers but by investors, not just on the quality of our products or their profits, but also on our values and how we holistically add value to the world. That is going to be a significant measuring stick as to whether or not people invest in a company. This will not necessarily be motivated by a desire by investors to solve world social problems. Instead, it will prompted by a growing belief among investors that in order to survive long term as profitable concerns, corporations will have to start thinking and acting in a socially-responsible way. Investors are realizing that if companies alienate the societies in which they operate, if they destroy the environment, sap precious natural resources, and ignore major social problems, they will alienate their customers and ultimately fail. A broad range of investors are going to say, "For the longevity of your business, I want to be sure you are sustainable as a business and you are operating in a sustainable manner." Only in that way will we be able to attract consumers and remain viable companies over time. And just as society expects big corporations to do more, so will the big companies expect more from their suppliers, prompting a chain reaction.

The answer is neither socialism nor the reckless capitalism that led to the world financial collapse in 2008 and the BP oil spill in 2010. The answer is Connected Capitalism.

Eighteenth-century philosopher Adam Smith once said, "It is not from the benevolence of the butcher, the brewer, or the baker that we expect our dinner, but from their regard for their own interest."

In the complex economy of the future, business interest and society's interests will become more closely aligned. Capitalism will have to be connected or it will not survive.

In conclusion, I would like to say that writing this book has been a positive catharsis. It has made me realize how truly lucky I am, born to the most caring, supportive parents, who created the opportunity to explore the world both physically and intellectually. Here I am sixty-eight years later with a wonderful nuclear family, Pamela, Cara, and her husband Zak, and our real joy, our grandson, Rory. I have visited 145 countries, met and supped with men and women of history, and, just as important, spent time with people of many cultures at every level of economic status. It is a life I could live all over again, even with the odd bad moments and the regrets. I have truly lived on the Coke side of life—happy, optimistic, and to the degree that it is in any way possible, innocent. My final career is well underway as I try to give back just a little to those less fortunate, who have been so kind to me.

INDEX